Praise for *Design Thi*

"Drawing on a wealth of research and real-world examples, David Dunne lays bare the tensions that face organizations when they try to shift to a more human-centric, design-driven way of working – and he provides insight into how to navigate those tensions to get results. A must-read for any leader determined to challenge the status quo within their organization."

Chris Ferguson, CEO, Bridgeable, and Adjunct Professor, Faculty of Law, University of Toronto

"David Dunne ... draws on years of research into how the theory [of design thinking] has been applied in organizations to explain the challenges, barriers, and potential pitfalls of design thinking, and to offer lessons for achieving success."

Peter Chadwick, IEDP

"*Design Thinking at Work* is a welcome contribution to our knowledge about how to actually make design thinking work and very valuable for those leading the way in organizations!"

Jeanne Liedtka, Professor of Business Adminstration, Darden School of Business, University of Virginia

design
thinking
at work

how innovative organizations
are embracing design

david dunne

UNIVERSITY OF TORONTO PRESS
Toronto Buffalo London

© University of Toronto Press 2018
Rotman-UTP Publishing
Toronto Buffalo London
utorontopress.com

Reprinted in paperback 2021

ISBN 978-1-4875-4878-0 (paper)   ISBN 978-1-4875-1379-5 (EPUB)
ISBN 978-1-4875-0170-9 (cloth)   ISBN 978-1-4875-1378-8 (PDF)

Publication cataloguing information is available from Library and Archives
Canada.

University of Toronto Press acknowledges the financial assistance to its
publishing program of the Canada Council for the Arts and the Ontario
Arts Council, an agency of the Government of Ontario.

Canada Council **Conseil des Arts**
for the Arts **du Canada**

ONTARIO ARTS COUNCIL
CONSEIL DES ARTS DE L'ONTARIO
an Ontario government agency
un organisme du gouvernement de l'Ontario

Funded by the   Financé par le
Government   gouvernement
of Canada   du Canada   Canada

This book is dedicated to my family:
Carol Ann;
Laurence and Liam;
Simon, Leila, and Lee;
and Gavin,
without whose love it would not have been possible.

contents

acknowledgments

The individuals I interviewed for this book were forthcoming, honest, realistic, and ultimately optimistic in their appraisal of design thinking in organizations. For reasons of space, not all were quoted in the book, though their contributions were nonetheless invaluable in helping shape my ideas. I am deeply indebted to Alex Ryan, Barb Korol, Mei Huang, and Wayne Crosby at Alberta CoLab; Jess Roberts at University of Minnesota College of Design; John Body, formerly at the Australian Tax Office, at ThinkPlace; Chris Ferguson at Bridgeable; Brandon Riddell at Canadian Tire; Craig Haney and Chris Plunkett at Communitech; Philip Rubel and Mikal Hallstrup at DesignIt; Ronna Chisolm at Dossier Creative; Mathew Chow, David Aycan, and Deb DeVries at IDEO; Joe Gerber and Dan Elitzer at IDEO CoLab; Xavier Debane and Rocky Jain at Manulife; Christian Bason, Jakob Schjørring, and Thomas Prehn at MindLab; Holly O'Driscoll and Cindy Tripp at Procter & Gamble; Mark Leung and Mihnea Galeteanu at Rotman; Judy Mellett, Chelsea Omel, Markus Grupp, Patrick Bach, and the Service Design team at TELUS; Brian Zubert at Thomson Reuters; Frido Smulders at TU Delft; Anna Kindler at the University of British Columbia; Wendy Mayer at Pfizer, and to several others who prefer to remain anonymous. Earlier interviews with experts, including Tim Brown, Jane Fulton

Suri, Jim Hackett, David Kelley, Larry Keeley, Vijay Kumar, Roger Martin, Whitney Mortimer, Donald Norman, Moura Quayle, Diego Rodriguez, and Patrick Whitney, helped me understand the nature of design thinking and its application. I am especially grateful to both Roger Martin and Patrick Whitney, who have been guiding lights in my design journey. Simon Dunne and Carol Ann Courneya reviewed an early draft and provided extremely helpful comments, as did two anonymous reviewers. Patrick Ho and the Railyard team at Dossier did wonderful work on cover designs. Finally, I owe special thanks to Brad Buie, at University of Victoria, for research support and insightful comments on several drafts; and to Jennifer DiDomenico, Manager, Social Sciences Acquisitions at University of Toronto Press, who could be counted on to provide much-needed clarity and helpful suggestions throughout.

design
thinking
at work

PART 1   **FRAMING DESIGN THINKING
IN ORGANIZATIONS**

thinking like a designer

How Design Keeps the Dutch Dry

Delft is a quaint Dutch city located about halfway between Rotterdam and The Hague. Sometimes called "little Amsterdam," its canals, churches, and narrow streets have a way of transporting you back in time (Figure 1.1a). If you didn't look too closely, you could be forgiven for thinking it unchanged since Johannes Vermeer immortalized it in his painting *View of Delft* in the 1600s (Figure 1.1b).

From time to time, the city's charms are less obvious. Winter storms batter the North Sea coast, bringing gale-force winds and driving rain, testing the patience of its residents – and the durability of their umbrellas, which tend to flip inside out in the high winds.

In a single week in March 2004, Gerwin Hoogendoorn lost three umbrellas to the elements. Frustrated by the experience, the industrial design student at the Delft University of Technology (TU Delft) set out to improve a product that had been essentially unchanged for 3,400 years. The ultimate result was Senz, a stormproof umbrella designed to withstand whatever nature could throw at the hapless Dutch pedestrian.

1.1a and 1.1b Delft today (left), and Vermeer's *View of Delft* (c. 1660)
Credit, 1.1a: Art Anderson, "Delft from the Feniks," Wikimedia Commons, CC BY-SA 3.0;
1.1b: Mauritshuis, The Hague. Photography: Margareta Svensson

Hoogendoorn explored everything about umbrellas: their tendency to flip inside out, to block visibility, to poke people in the eye. Umbrellas were a boring utilitarian product that didn't fulfil their function well – so boring, in fact, that Hoogendoorn had to endure the ridicule of his fellow design students, Gerard Kool and Philip Hess, for even working on such a product.

His early ideas included a magnetic field to repel the rain and a helicopter-like device attached to the user's head. Eventually, however, he focused on the aerodynamics of umbrellas. With no background in aerodynamics, he sought out the help of university contacts with expertise in the field. To build prototypes, he bought a couple of umbrellas, tore them apart, and rebuilt them (Figure 1.2). He tested his ideas through computer simulation, wind tunnels, and "in-use" tests (i.e., taking them out in the Dutch rain).

With Kool and Hess – who, by now, had begun to come around to the idea – Hoogendoorn founded Senz in 2005. The first Senz

1.2 Hoogendoorn works on the Senz umbrella
Credit: www.senz.com / Production: VLA Productions / Client: Industrial Design Engineering, TU Delft

1.3 The Senz umbrella
Credit: www.senz.com

umbrella was launched in November 2006; its original, quirky design (Figure 1.3) captured the public imagination, and the initial stock of 10,000 units sold out in nine days. In its first year, Senz won almost every major design award and went global in 2007.

Hoogendoorn's design school, TU Delft, is a venerated institution in the design world. A few years ago, I spent a sabbatical there, during which I experienced the Dutch rain on more than one occasion. As a former marketing executive and a professor of marketing at the Rotman School of Management in Toronto, I had been on a journey to explore "design thinking" for some years. I wanted to know everything I could about design and design thinking. What was design thinking anyway, and how was it different from any other kind of thinking? How was it practised in business and the public sector, and what happened when it was?

I felt the best way to conduct this exploration was to immerse myself in the world of design. I hung out with designers. I read deeply about design and design theory. I worked with designers on projects. I talked with designers, design educators, and design thinkers in organizations. I taught business strategy to designers and design thinking to executives. My design journey led me not only to Delft but also to many more places around the world.

I found that designers look at the world in a distinct and interesting way. I found not just creativity but also curiosity, rigour, and discipline. I found some answers – and many more questions.

To a designer like Hoogendoorn, what was design thinking? On the face of it, his idea of design sounds fairly simple: "I think good design is an object or a service that exceeds the user's expectation," he says in a promotional video.[1]

But even if we had a good way of understanding what the user expects, how would we know which problem to work on? Flimsy umbrellas are just one of those everyday problems that seem to plague us. We take such problems for granted and don't think much about them, much less about solving them. Hoogendoorn's genius seemed to be in *selecting* the problem as much as in solving it.

Once he had decided to work on the problem, he went back and forth, drawing things, building rough models, testing them, redefining the problem, moving on from ridiculous ideas to more practical ones, and learning as he went along. His approach was exploratory, driven by curiosity.

For companies that make consumer products, the ability of designers like Hoogendoorn to find genius in the everyday is inspiring – and perhaps a little disconcerting. Hoogendoorn approached Impliva, a major umbrella distributor, and was turned down before embarking on his own project. It seems to suggest that designers see possibilities that companies don't see.

Many organizations have taken this to heart, wondering what the "secret sauce" of design might be, and whether it could be applied to their own problems. Design thinking has been touted as an answer to this question and has grown from a fringe activity to a central weapon in the problem-solver's arsenal. An army of consultants and management gurus now promote it as the long-awaited answer to the problem of innovation in organizations.

If only it were that simple.

Most of my career to date has been spent in large organizations. Exciting as design thinking is – and I still find myself passionate about it – it is not easy to apply. As I have explored design thinking, I have encountered many with a similar passion who struggle to make it work in a large organization. It is such a different way of looking at problems that it can pose a challenge to the prevailing culture and approach.

I've found that organizational design thinkers face common problems, tensions that they have to manage in order to survive.

Fortunately, some are not merely surviving but are thriving. How they do so is the subject of this book.

The book is divided into three parts, and you'll find a roadmap in Figure 1.4. In part 1, Framing Design Thinking in Organizations, I will discuss what design thinking actually means (chapter 1) and how it fits into large organizations in the private, public, and not-for-profit sectors. I've found that design thinkers in organizations face three tensions: the Tension of *Inclusion*, the Tension of *Disruption*,

Part 1: Framing Design Thinking in Organizations

Chapter 1: Thinking Like a Designer
What is design thinking, and what's interesting about it?

Chapter 2: The Adoption of Design Thinking
How has design thinking caught on in organizations, and what are the challenges?

Part 2: The Three Tensions

Chapter 3: The Tension of Inclusion
How have design thinkers navigated the challenge of being "inside" or "outside" the organization?

Chapter 4: The Tension of Disruption
How have design thinkers pursued disruptive innovations while meeting demands for incremental change?

Chapter 5: The Tension of Perspective
How have design thinkers taken a user perspective while innovating at the system level?

Part 3: Reframing Design Thinking for Your Organization

Chapter 6: Reframing Design Thinking
What does the experience of these organizations tell us about how to deal with the three tensions?

Chapter 7: Where Do You Begin? Building Your Design Thinking Program
What decisions do you need to make if you're starting up a design thinking program in your organization?

1.4 A roadmap of this book

and the Tension of *Perspective* (chapter 2). If you're new to the notion of design thinking or would like to know more about it, read chapter 1; if you're already familiar with it and your primary interest is in how it works in organizations, go to chapter 2.

Part 2, The Three Tensions, explores each of the three tensions in turn, looking at how organizations manage their way through them and how the best design-thinking programs have learned to *reframe* their work to deal with them (chapters 3, 4, and 5). This is the part you want if you're interested in exploring in depth the world of design thinking in organizations.

The final part, Reframing Design Thinking for Your Organization, draws the insights from the research together (chapter 6) and provides a roadmap for starting and managing a design-thinking program in your organization (chapter 7). If your main question is "What do I do next?" this is the part for you.

I'll begin with an overview of the idea of design thinking.

Design … and Design *Thinking*

As an idea, design thinking is tough to pin down. That's because design itself is both ubiquitous and multifaceted.

Whether consciously or not, human beings are always designing something. Only nature in its purest form has not been designed – and in the modern world, even nature is affected by design, through environmental damage or, more hopefully, measures to protect the environment. Design is everywhere: in the hat we wear, the flowerbed in our front garden, the paper cup we drink from.

Typically, though, we don't think of design this way. We have design schools, where students learn a set of techniques and methods; we have "star" designers like Rem Koolhaas, Dieter Rams, or Karl Lagerfeld; we have their classic designs, like the Eames chair (Figure 1.5a) or Philippe Starck's Alessi citrus squeezer (Figure 1.5b).

Design has become a conscious, self-aware activity, rooted in science – the science of making things work – but has also been elevated to an art form.

Some of this refinement of design carries with it more than a hint of arrogance. The architect Denys Lasdun argued that "our job is to give the client … *not* what he wants, but what he never dreamed he wanted."[2] Star designers seem to define what is "cool," and we follow.

Many practising designers are uncomfortable with this elitist notion of design and argue for a concept of design that puts users, not designers, first. This is called user-centred, or human-centred, design.

"Design thinking" extends from this concept of user-centred design into a comprehensive innovation process that considers the full range of contextual factors. Tim Brown, CEO of design firm IDEO, argues that design thinking integrates business strategy and technology with the needs of the user:

> [Design Thinking is] a discipline that uses the designer's sensibility and methods to match people's needs with what is *technologically feasible* and what a *viable business strategy* can convert into *customer value and market opportunity*.[3]

Many business problems are hard to define, and design thinking offers a kind of toolkit to help you work through the ambiguity. In this way of thinking, design thinking is a *process*: a collection of things that you do to innovate. Through methods like ethnographic research, you explore users' lives and underlying needs; you use

1.5a and 1.5b Eames chair (top); Alessi
citrus squeezer (right)

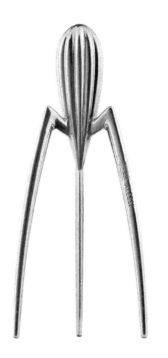

frameworks[4] to define problems and analyse the data; you study competitive offerings and strategies; you develop an intimate understanding of technology and the company's resources. You build prototypes as you go.

But where do you begin? Some versions give the starting point as user desirability, but it isn't that simple. Design thinking is not a linear exercise in which one step neatly follows another; nor is it really circular. Research with expert designers shows that they go back-and-forth in an *iterative* process,[5] going from analysis to prototype, back to analysis, to data collection, and so on. To an outsider, it can look chaotic and unpredictable. To a designer, where you start doesn't matter.

Design can be seen as a *reflective* process, in which the "situation talks back" – that is, responds to the designer's efforts and thereby provides feedback for the next iteration.[6] Like Hoogendoorn's back-and-forth development of the Senz umbrella, design is about exploration.

Yet for many designers, something is lost in this way of thinking. They see design thinking as much more than a set of tools; rather, it is a distinct way of being, an attitude, or an orientation in the world. Design researcher Kees Dorst suggests that "design is a way of looking, of being more actively involved in the world than most people. You are never content with how things appear. It is impossible to be bored when you are a designer."[7]

Management professors Richard Boland and Fred Collopy compare a *design attitude* with a *decision attitude*:

> A decision attitude ... assumes it is easy to come up with alternatives to consider, but difficult to choose among them ... the design attitude towards problem solving, in contrast, assumes that it is difficult to design a good alternative, but once you have developed a good one, the decision about which alternative to select becomes trivial.[8]

What Boland and Collopy, as well as others, argue is that design is about how you inherently respond, emotionally and attitudinally, to problems. It's an attitude of curiosity, openness, and a willingness to play.

This way of approaching problems is very different from the standard managerial mindset. One designer I interviewed some years ago put it this way:

> [Design thinking is] a way of approaching problems in the world that begins from a point of optimism, that there is a solution, and it's a matter of us reaching it. It builds on that with this idea of "mind of a child," [the] ability to be open to whatever the world is going to tell you, and coupling that with an attitude of wisdom.[9]

While design thinking has a toolkit, a toolkit alone won't make you a design thinker. In its essence it is about iteration, experimentation, and reflection. More than that, it is a mindset: playful, tolerant of ambiguity, and open to learning. These qualities have captured the notice of organizations.

Before we discuss design thinking's impact on organizations, let's take look more closely at its components.

A Deeper Look at Design Thinking

Design is often associated with creativity: for many people, the image that comes to mind is a group of hipsters, sitting on bean-bag chairs and papering the wall with Post-Its. Creativity is very much an element – but it enters the process in many ways, and it's a mistake to think of design thinking as just a form of brainstorming. It's better thought of as *an integrated and disciplined innovation process that builds creative insight from deep knowledge.*

A good deal has been written about design thinking, and there are many versions of how it works. Although their features, labelling, and emphasis differ, they tend to have three important things in common: experimentation, deep understanding, and creative reframing.

The first of the three is *experimentation*. Looking back at Hoogendoorn's approach to the umbrella problem, it's interesting to think about what he did *not* do.

Design Thinking and Other Types of Thinking

Hoogendoorn was interested in physical, tangible objects rather than abstract ideas. Driven by curiosity, his first instinct was to dive in and try something – to experiment. Experimentation is a central idea in both design and science – but with a very different meaning.

In 2007, Charles Owen, a professor at the IIT Institute of Design in Chicago, looked at how creative thinkers in different fields approached problems. He mapped fields on two axes: on one, a field could range from *analytic*, concerned with "finding," to *synthetic*, concerned with "making" or inventing. On the other, a field could range from *symbolic*, concerned with abstraction, to *real*, concerned with physical things. The analytic/synthetic axis was about process, or ways of working, while the symbolic/real axis was about content.

For Owen, both science and design were types of creative thinking. Science was about discovery and located mainly in the symbolic/analytic domain. Art was symbolic and had elements of analysis and synthesis. Clinical medicine was rooted in the real world and analytic in nature.

Sitting in the synthetic/real domain, designers were concerned with *integrating* things – putting them together – rather than breaking them apart by analysing them, and with reality as distinct from art, which dealt with symbols.

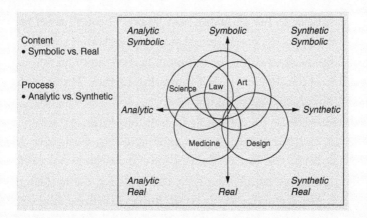

Charles Owen's conception of creative thinking in different fields.
Credit: Design Research Society/Charles Owen

He did not – at least initially – analyse the market. He did not identify a market segment, analyse competitive strategy, do pro forma financials. Nor did he develop a General Theory of Umbrellas. Instead, he tinkered: he bought two umbrellas, pulled them apart and rebuilt them; he drew mock designs; he tested his models in wind tunnels and with users on the street. As he did so, his ideas became more refined and focused.

Hoogendoorn's trial-and-error approach allowed him to learn more about the problem and the issues involved in solving it as he went along. Compared with a "linear" process that moves systematically from problem to solution, a designer tries things out, moving from problem straight to solution and back again. This is also the spirit of brainstorming, in which a team suspends criticism while exploring solutions – but it goes much further.

Designers experiment constantly, jumping from early conceptions of the problem straight to sketches, back to the problem, to rough mockups, back to the problem, and so on. Through *rapid prototyping*, the designer makes rough physical models of a solution, without taking too much time for refinement, making them just finished enough to see if they are worth pursuing further. These prototypes are critical vehicles for thinking.

By representing the problem in tangible form, prototypes play a role in clarifying the choices available. As designers Marion Buchenau and Jane Fulton Suri point out, making can either *narrow* the options or *broaden* them:[10] "The tools we use to design, such as prototypes, influence the way we think. Solutions, and probably even imagination, are inspired and limited by the prototyping tools we have at our disposal." In his classic 1983 book, *The Reflective Practitioner*,[11] Donald Schön explored the interplay between doing and thinking. Schön set out to discover how professionals thought about their work. Starting from the idea that professionals use "reflection-in-action" – more than improvisation, a seamless flow between thinking and doing – and he explored how this approach is used in design and other fields.

Schön described how this flow occurred in an interaction between an architecture student, Petra, and her instructor, Quist, as he commented on, and wrote and drew over, Petra's initial design. Thought and action were closely interwoven:

> The verbal and non-verbal dimensions are closely connected. Quist's lines
> are unclear in their reference except insofar as he says what they mean.

His words are obscure except insofar as Petra can connect them with the lines of the drawing. His talk is full of dychtic* utterances – "here," "this," "that" – which Petra can interpret only by observing his movements.[12]

Kees Dorst and Nigel Cross also described this back-and-forth interplay between thought and action, describing it as "co-evolution of problem-space and solution-space." By studying the thoughts of designers as they worked through a problem of designing a waste receptacle for Dutch Railways, they found that the designers worked by trying a solution, reflecting on the result, and trying again. Each time the designers tried something, they learned a little more about the problem.[13]

In a sense, the designers "spoke" to the problem, and the problem "talked back" – in Schön's words, it was a "reflective conversation with the situation"[14] – and the communication medium was the prototype. For this reason, design researchers sometimes call prototypes "boundary objects" as they help transcend communication barriers.

Learning by Prototyping

Making is about understanding problems and solving them at the same time. Each attempt raises new questions about the nature, scope, and impact of the problem. Making is as much about learning and discovery as it is about problem solving.

Because making helps you learn, you need to make as much as you can, think about it, and let the results influence the next

---

*   I am unable to find a dictionary definition of the word "dychtic"; Schön seems to have invented it. In this context, "verbal" seems a good substitute. The main point is that Quist's words are not enough to convey his meaning.

thing you make. Rapid prototyping is the process of making rough, frequent, low-fidelity solution attempts.

The prototype is an attempt to solve the problem, but its main value is as a vehicle for learning. It's rapid because the more you make, the more you learn – and the more you build the energy of creative flow in a team.

At heart, designers are tinkerers who like to play with ideas by trying them out. The library at TU Delft in the Netherlands provides a "tinker table," where design students can scratch their itch to build things.

For designers, a prototype is a means to an end. The prototype itself has no value, but the learning gained from it has potentially a great deal of it. The success or failure of the prototype does

The tinker table in the TU Delft's library

not matter: prototypes are produced rapidly at low resolution and tossed around casually – as a way of asserting that these are not objects of inherent value but vehicles for developing a better understanding of the problem and those affected by it.

The second distinctive characteristic of design thinking is *deep understanding* of the context, with the user as the central focus.

Because designers are concerned with making things that are tangible, real, and (usually) useful, it stands to reason that they have a deep understanding of what's involved in using them. Don't they?

You would think so, but look at some of the objects we're saddled with. The plastic pack of nuts that you bought as you rushed to your flight – and that you can't open without a knife or a pair of scissors. (Try getting either of those on a plane.) In desperation, you rip it open with your teeth, and most of the nuts end up at your feet.

Or the sophisticated camera you bought at great expense last year that has hundreds of features that you'll never use, because by the time you've figured them out, the beautiful sunset has passed and you can't see the controls in the dark. And so on. Evidently, not all designers think of users a great deal.

Disconnection from users reached crisis proportions in the early 1980s, when personal computers were in their infancy. Designed by geeks for geeks, each generation of computer became more complex and less accessible to the ordinary user.

Several things happened as a result. Seeing users' frustration, the human-computer interface (HCI) movement sought to bring an understanding of human behaviour into computer development.[15]

Apple, famously, launched the Macintosh computer, with its "1984" commercial depicting a dystopian technology-based dictatorship and the implication that the machines – or at least those made by its nemesis IBM – were taking over.

In 1988, Donald Norman, in *The Psychology of Everyday Things*,[16] argued for user-centred design – the idea that design should focus on the experience of use and make it intuitive and clear. Things should be visible, and the user should know what actions are possible at any given moment.

It may seem obvious that design should embrace users' experiences, but not everyone feels that users should have an important say in design. After all, designers are concerned with things that don't yet exist, and users typically understand only what they already know. Steve Jobs was famous for his disdain for giving users a voice in design. "A lot of times, people don't know what they want until you show it to them," he said in 1997.[17]

Actually, there is not much to disagree with in Jobs's statement. Ask users what they want, and you will usually get a blank stare. We tolerate all kinds of imperfection in our daily lives, without really being aware of it. Most of it is just not that important to us – when your umbrella flips, you get wet, complain, and assume that umbrellas will always be that way.

Design thinkers consult users – but not by simply asking them what they want. They look for problems that we take for granted, assume to be insoluble, or just fail to notice. They seek to understand the *context* surrounding the use of existing products and why they work – or don't work – in that context.

This kind of research can expose what might be missing, even if users aren't aware that it's missing. Craig Wynett, director of Corporate New Ventures at Procter & Gamble (P&G), described how the company used ethnographic methods* in 1994 to design what ultimately became the Swiffer floor cleaner:

> The team set out as design anthropologists to watch how people cleaned their kitchen floor … We visited 18 homes in Cincinnati and Boston, spending about an hour and a half in each … Mostly we just watched, although when we did not understand why [the homemakers] did something, we asked them to explain. We took notes and video recorded the entire process so that we could analyze it later.[18]

The team found that floor cleaning was a complex process that involved multiple steps. Before cleaning even began, furniture had to be moved, the floor swept or vacuumed, the pail filled with clean water and detergent, and so on. Floor cleaning was a dirty process, so the homemakers changed their clothes before taking on the task. By analysing this behaviour in depth, along with the scientific aspects of floor cleaning, the team developed a set of requirements for the design. Wrote Wynett, "We were looking for a solution that: works for both sweeping and mopping; does not require you to clean the broom or mop after cleaning the floor; is clean to use and doesn't make you want to wear old clothes; is quick and fun so people want to clean more and can have cleaner homes." Ultimately, after several failed ideas and prototypes, the Swiffer Duster was launched in 1999, and the Swiffer WetJet in 2001. Swiffer is one of P&G's most successful new product introductions, with sales of more than $1 billion a year.

The P&G design team, as design anthropologists, observed and interviewed users. Others go further and bring users directly into the

---

* Ethnographic research is the study of people and cultures. The term is used pretty loosely in design, to mean qualitative research on individual users and their context of use.

User Experience and Driverless Cars

With the rapid development of cars that drive themselves, at least one design expert is sounding a note of caution. Donald Norman has long been an outspoken advocate of bringing user experience into design.

Norman argues that cars that are mostly, but not fully, automated pose a danger to drivers and other road users because drivers do not intervene in time in case of emergency. "When there is little to do, attention wanders," he wrote in the *San Diego Union-Tribune* in 2015.

Tesla's Autopilot for the Model S provides the automated ability to steer, change lanes, and manage speed, using digital control of motors, brakes, and steering. However, according to Norman, Tesla had not taken enough trouble to understand the real-world experience of users before introducing Autopilot: "Tesla is being reckless. From what I can tell, Tesla has no understanding of how real drivers operate and they do not understand the need for careful testing. So [Tesla] release [Autopilot], and then they have to pull back."

It is easy to become so obsessed with the attractions of new technology that one loses sight of user experience. Norman's point is that careful research into the actual, not assumed, experience of users is a prerequisite for effective design.

Designers ignore users at their peril – and, in some cases, at users' peril. In July 2016, a Tesla Model S under Autopilot ploughed into an eighteen-wheel truck in Williston, Florida, killing the car's only occupant, Joshua Brown. Tesla claimed that its Autopilot technology was not at fault. In an interview with *Fast*

Company Design in 2017, Norman said, "I think Tesla is starting to learn its lesson. It's unfortunate it had to learn it the hard way."

The Tesla crash in Williston, Florida. Credit: https://www.flickr.com/ photos/ntsb/35366284636/in/photostream/; public domain under Creative Commons. National Transportation Safety Board; photo by Florida Highway Patrol Investigators

---

design process. Many design projects, especially for complex products and services, follow a "participatory design" model in which users are not merely observed but are invited into the design team.

The third distinctive element of design thinking is *creatively reframing* the problem. To reframe a problem is to ask a different question, to see it from a different perspective.

Some years ago, I led a workshop on design thinking at a Toronto hospital. A group of doctors and nurses came to the workshop with a problem that had great importance for them: the difficulty in finding a private spot, in a crowded emergency department, to discuss patients' problems in confidence. The solutions to a problem like this are fairly obvious: put up walls or partitions, create white noise, and so on.

Mihnea Galeteanu, a graduate student I had planted in the team, saw things differently, even a little naïvely. The discussion went like this:

Galeteanu: Why is the emergency department so crowded?
Other team members: Because patients are waiting, with their families, to be seen.
Galeteanu: Why are they waiting in the emergency department?
Other team members: Because we've told them to wait, so they will be available when we call them.
Galeteanu: Can they be available without actually being in the emergency department?

The team acknowledged that some patients and their families could indeed leave and come back when it was time for a doctor to see them. Instead of "How can we get more privacy?" the problem was reframed to "How might we reduce overcrowding?"

This reframing yielded an interesting set of solutions, including pagers and an app that allowed those awaiting treatment to wander in the hospital's cafes and shopping area, or further afield – thereby dealing with the original problem of overcrowding while making patients happier and raising revenue for the hospital.

Albert Einstein is often quoted as saying, "If I had an hour to solve a problem I'd spend 55 minutes thinking about the problem and 5 minutes thinking about solutions." While Einstein may never have actually said this,[19] the idea of thinking carefully about the problem before jumping to solutions is nonetheless characteristic of design thinking.

Einstein could have thought about the problem in three ways: by deductive, inductive, or abductive reasoning. *Deductive* reasoning is about applying a general rule to a specific instance: had he reasoned deductively, he would have observed the situation and looked at what necessarily followed from it. If all umbrellas flip inside out in windy conditions, and Einstein has been out on a windy day with his umbrella, then his damaged umbrella must be due to the wind.

Inductive reasoning is reasoning that takes you from a specific case to a general rule: if windy conditions caused Einstein's umbrella to flip inside out last week, then he should stay indoors as his umbrella is likely to flip.

Deductive and inductive reasoning have been recognized by philosophers for many centuries. In 1903, Charles Sanders Peirce described *abductive* reasoning,[20] and this type of thinking gets interesting from a design perspective. To reason abductively is to infer something: if Einstein had a better umbrella, perhaps it would not flip, and he could go out. So abductive reasoning is about *creating possibilities*.

A different perspective can create possibilities by transforming a problem. At the University of Technology, Sydney, Designing Out Crime (http://designingoutcrime.com/) works to bring design innovation to crime and social problems. In partnership with the New South Wales Department of Justice, the centre uses a method called frame creation to think deeply through problems.

In one case, the group worked on the problems in a Sydney neighbourhood called Kings Cross. The area had several nightclubs and was the scene of a good deal of alcohol-fuelled crime. On a weekend, it attracted up to 30,000 people, 75 percent of whom were between the ages of fifteen and thirty. The authorities had tried increasing the police presence, installing CCTV cameras, arresting troublemakers, and similar measures, but the problem persisted.

The Designing Out Crime team focused its attention on framing the problem – as they put it, "taking a walk around the problem" – by exploring its context and different ways of looking at it. The team's research showed that weekend visitors to Kings Cross were not criminals, but were ordinary young people looking for a good time. Yet because the area was not equipped to manage 30,000 people, trouble was sure to follow.

Existing solutions tended to criminalize the visitors by focusing on surveillance and restrictions. Instead, the team used the metaphor of a large-scale music festival as a lens, reinterpreting the issue as one of crowd management rather than crime. This reframing of Kings Cross as an "event" led to a very different set of solutions, including public urinals, street ambassadors, and artistic light installations.

Reframing has been described as *seeing, thinking, and acting* in a feedback loop to yield a novel stance about the issue. Designers look to identify a "problem space," which in turn determines the scope and nature of possible solutions. For some design theorists, rather than random brainstorming, framing is a core design skill,[21] where designers' true creativity lies.

Seen from this perspective, Hoogendoorn's magnetic fields and helicopter-like devices were his way of exploring the problem, initially framing it as "keeping dry" without confining himself to umbrellas. Eventually, his exploration led him back to the possibility of making a better umbrella.

These three distinctive elements – experimentation, deep understanding, and creative reframing – are not separate from each other but work together like the gears of an engine. While all three parts are represented in design thinking, there is no defined starting point.

Hoogendoorn began by taking umbrellas apart and putting them back together. The Swiffer team analysed the user's experience of floor cleaning. Designing Out Crime found a creative analogy to represent the problem and take an alternative point of view. All experimented, explored user experience, and reframed – but not necessarily in that order. This combination of depth, creativity, and flexibility makes design thinking adaptable to a wide range of difficult problems in business, government, and society.

The Impact of Design Thinking: Wicked Problems

Charles Eames (1907–88), the renowned American designer, was once asked, "What are the boundaries of design?" to which he answered, "What are the boundaries of problems?"[22] Design thinking has shown that it can be helpful across a wide range of issues in the private, public and non-profit sectors, with a particular focus on innovation.

If design thinking can be applied to all kinds of problems, it has advantages with what are called *wicked problems*, for which the biggest issue is deciding just what the problem is – or, in design terminology, framing the problem space. The iterative, reflective nature of design thinking makes it particularly applicable to problems of this type.

Wicked problems are chronic, beyond complex, with no clear boundaries or solutions. As design theorist Horst Rittel argued in the 1960s,[23] they are a "class of social system problems which are ill-formulated, where the information is confusing, where there are many clients and decision makers with conflicting values, and where the ramifications in the whole system are thoroughly confusing."

Though Rittel was talking about social problems, such as managing the economy or the education system, professional designers would recognize in his words a description of problems they work with on a daily basis. Design theorists like Richard Buchanan argued that because design thinking was both *universal* in scope and tasked with inventing *particular* things, it was uniquely suited to wicked problems.[24] Like Hoogendoorn, designers had to look at a problem through an extremely broad lens but end up devising a specific solution to it.

While Rittel was defining wicked problems in society, management theorists were also recognized the wickedness of the problems confronting managers.[25] By the 2000s, globalization and technological advances had brought complexity and ambiguity, and "wicked problems" seemed an apt description of the challenges managers regularly faced. While designers were equipped to deal with them (albeit imperfectly), managers struggled with a linear approach that started from the assumption of a well-defined problem space.

Design thinking offered a way through these wicked problems. Solving them turned on understanding the nature and scope of the problem rather than accepting conventional ways of framing it: this was the strength of design thinking's iterative approach.

In the early 2000s, I was on faculty at the Rotman School of Management at the University of Toronto. Roger Martin, its dean, was arguing that most businesses were too focused on analytical thinking and thus were refining current knowledge and producing small improvements to the status quo. I was intrigued.

Martin showed how some businesses successfully innovated by applying design thinking. In a 2009 book,[26] he used case studies from Procter & Gamble, Cirque du Soleil, RIM, and others to argue that businesses face "mysteries" that do not have an obvious solution and need to find ways of innovating to deal with them. Design, for Martin, was "the next competitive advantage." For me, it was a new way of thinking about educating business students to deal with the wicked problems they would face when they graduated.

The public sector also began to see the value of design thinking for wicked social problems. From Denmark to the United States to Singapore, governments experimented with design "labs," usually on a small scale at first.

In a 2013 article,[27] Christian Bason, then director of MindLab, the Danish government's design thinking lab, argued the case for design thinking in government. However, he saw several challenges. While setting up a new lab was feasible, embedding the approach in government was a different matter. Governments did not have the right skills; the consulting market was still not developed; and the hierarchical nature of government tended to have difficulties with a citizen-centred approach in which multiple, diverse stakeholders needed to be engaged.

The U.S. government's experience with design thinking was a case in point. In 2012, the Office of Personnel Management (OPM) spent $1.5 million to build and staff its innovation lab.[28] Conceived as a Silicon Valley–style technology hub, it was originally established to rebuild the OPM's website but soon found itself dealing with a broad range of problems across the OPM.

While there was a good deal of enthusiasm at the OPM, the General Accounting Office (GAO) was less impressed. It found that the OPM's innovation centre lacked a rigorous evaluation framework and argued that it needed to develop clear, specific outcome measures.[29]

Bason was nonetheless an optimist: seeing the growth in interest in public-sector design thinking around the world, he concluded his article with his belief that the glass is more than half-full for design-led innovation in government. MindLab, for its part, was making a difference with projects that included rethinking waste management, reducing tensions between inmates and guards in prisons, and transforming services for mentally disabled adults.

Global poverty is perhaps the wickedest of wicked problems. In 2014, the United Nations Development Programme also saw the value of design thinking in dealing with wicked social problems: "The goal of design thinking is to equip governments with innovative approaches to face contemporary challenges such as interconnected and diffused economic and social patterns, more complex problems, blurred governance boundaries, and reduced trust in public action."[30] The less-structured world of social innovation has also begun to embrace design thinking. In 2012, the MaRS Solutions Lab in Toronto published a set of case studies of twenty-three innovation labs around the world. The design firm IDEO has established IDEO.org, devoted to designing "products, services, and experiences to improve the lives of people in poor and vulnerable communities."

One example is d.light (www.dlight.com), a social enterprise focused on providing affordable social energy to the developing world. Its product range includes solar lighting and power products, as well as power systems for home, work, and schoolwork. D.light was born at Stanford University's "d.school" design thinking lab. Its founder, Sam Goldman, commented, "The passion and the design thinking initially forged at the d.school continue to drive the culture and mission of d.light. Solar lighting is just the beginning; we see ourselves as a provider of renewable energy in the developing world, and we'll continue to expand our product solutions and distribution networks in the coming years." There is no shortage of examples like these. The adherents of design thinking, among whom I count myself, argue that its ability to draw out human ingenuity, grounded in deep research, makes it hugely beneficial in tackling the toughest of problems.

Yet while its benefits are undeniable, its implementation in the real world of organizations has not always gone well.

Design Thinking in Organizations

Design thinking initiatives, mostly in the form of "innovation labs," are popping up in organizations everywhere. What is less common – because it is infinitely more difficult – is the adoption of a design mindset.

The designer's openness, curiosity, and fluidity sit uncomfortably in the rigid processes of large organizations; disruptive innovation consumes scarce resources and can test the patience of organizations; and it can be difficult to sustain a user-centred point of view. These challenges reflect the three tensions of design thinking in organizations: the Tension of *Inclusion*, the Tension of *Disruption*, and the Tension of *Perspective*. The best design thinking programs have learned to *reframe* their work to deal with these tensions.

In the next chapter, I'll talk about the organizations I've spoken with, why they are interested in design thinking and what they want from it, and I'll describe the three tensions they deal with. In chapters 3, 4. and 5 I will explore each of the tensions in turn. Chapter 6 draws together the lessons they've learned and suggests how design thinking might be reframed to work in *your* organization, while chapter 7 gives some specific guidelines for setting up your own design thinking program.

It is an exaggeration to say that design thinking is the answer to the world's problems. Yet across the private, public, and non-profit sectors, we hear the echoes of Eames's rhetorical question about the boundaries of problems: because wicked problems have no boundaries, we can expect to see design thinking's influence grow. Design can take us far beyond a wet day in Delft – but the essence of design thinking is beneath the umbrella, in the *mindset* that invented Senz.

the adoption of design thinking

A Design Journey

April 2007 was raw and frigid in Chicago. As I looked south towards the Loop, the majestic statue of Ceres atop the Board of Trade seemed to tell me to stand and face the cold like a good Midwesterner. I hurried across to 350 North LaSalle St, home of the Illinois Institute of Technology Institute of Design.

If you've visited Chicago and explored its stunning architecture, you'll know that it is a city that pays attention to design. Among its many famous institutions is the Illinois Institute of Technology. Its main campus (Figures 2.1a and 2.1b), itself an architectural masterpiece designed by landmark architects Ludwig Mies van der Rohe and Rem Koolhaas, is some way south of the city.

IIT's design school, the IIT Institute of Design – ID for short – was housed at that time in an office tower, a landmark building in its own right, located just north of the Chicago River.

ID's annual strategy conference was a unique fusion of design and business, and I had been attending for some years. Its dean, Patrick Whitney, quiet and unassuming, spoke with great eloquence about the power and potential of design thinking in business. When

2.1a and 2.1b At IIT Campus: Crown Hall by Mies van der Rohe (top), and Rem Koolhaas's Campus Center

he invited me to spend a few weeks as a research fellow at ID, the chance – to learn about design by hanging out with designers – seemed too good to pass up. In later years, I would build on what I learned at ID by teaching at other design schools and working with design firms.

Innovation and design had been part of my life for decades. As a former innovation manager in the packaged-goods industry, I had worked closely with creative people to design products, packaging, communications, and services. As a professor at the Rotman School of Management in Toronto in the early 2000s, I was exposed to design thinking as a way of approaching the world. I saw great possibilities for this concept in management education.[1] My visit to ID, however, gave me new respect for a process that, till then, I barely understood.

ID, founded in 1937 as the New Bauhaus, considers itself a "methods" school, emphasizing analysis, synthesis, and structured thinking as cornerstones of effective design. Its students are taught hundreds of tools to think systematically through problems and support creativity.[2] Design, I learned, is not just a creative enterprise but a rigorous one too.

In Chicago, ID students introduced me to the local Irish pub, Fadó. Over pints of Guinness, they would share with me their energy and enthusiasm for design thinking – and their worries about finding jobs. For all the hype, there wasn't much traction for design thinking in business at the time, and I left Chicago with many questions about how design thinking could ever be adopted more broadly. In later years, I would see many organizations embrace design thinking. Yet while some of these initiatives succeeded, many floundered.

Some designers were accusing business gurus of turning design thinking into a management fad, and I began to wonder whether, for all its appeal, it had been oversold. Perhaps organizations were embracing it as the next big thing without truly understanding it?

Or perhaps, in spite of the best efforts of its advocates, design thinking was just too difficult for organizations, too great a departure from normal business thinking. Managers were being advised to think like designers,[3] but was this realistic?

I was to find elements of both: design thinking had indeed been oversold and misunderstood, and it was not easy for managers to get their heads around it. But it *was* possible. Some initiatives were surviving in the face of difficult challenges, while some were even thriving. These organizations were managing the three tensions of design thinking, and the best were redefining innovation by reframing these tensions.

Designers and the Design Thinking "Fad"

Designers have long known that they have a distinct way of thinking and so coined the term "design thinking" long before it caught the attention of the business community. But the aggressive selling of design thinking seemed for many designers to trivialize their profession, packaging it in an easily digestible form for managers.

Many organizations have been seduced by a dumbed-down version of design thinking, thinking of it as wild idea generation but passing over the deep analysis and reflection that are needed to come up with these ideas. One frustrated designer I interviewed, who preferred to remain anonymous, lamented the "lack of attention span" in his organization, saying, "They're not willing to sit in the question, not willing to chew on it a little or revisit for a while ... They really quickly jump to 'We want this finished, we want to move on,' as opposed to actually taking the time to prototype, reframe, go through the iterations."

Ultimately, the trivialization of design thinking got it into trouble. When it did not reach the impossible heights claimed for it – literally, to change the world – some wrote it off. In 2011, Bruce Nussbaum, assistant managing editor of *Businessweek* and one of design thinking's erstwhile advocates, dismissed it as a "failed experiment."[4]

This, I felt, was unfair. Yet for a while, I was uncomfortable with the term "design thinking" and took steps to avoid using it. One reason for my discomfort was the reaction of some in the design community to the term: to them, design thinking had always been there and was part of the air they breathed. While some appreciated the attention, others resented the hype from what they saw as management *arrivistes*.

In my early research, I ran into quite a bit of suspicion as a businessperson with an interest in design thinking. One innovation consultant I interviewed told me, "[Design thinking is] just too simplistic. I'm kind of getting crotchety – I hope never defensive – but crotchety, if you oversimplify this subtle story."

On another occasion, a prominent design researcher dropped into my office at a design school. On hearing that I was a businessperson, he smiled and said, "Oh, so you're one of those people who think it's just about Post-Its."

My gaze fell on a couple of pads of brightly coloured Post-Its on my desk. Ouch.

As many designers saw it, the business community's "discovery" of design thinking and its subsequent popularization cheapened the creative and rigorous work they were doing and passed over the rich body of knowledge that had been developed about the field.

Design theorists Petra Badke-Schaub, Norbert Roozenburg, and Carlos Cardoso argued that the hype around design thinking had diluted its meaning. While design thinking has a strong tradition in the design field, Badke-Schaub and her colleagues claimed that its business proponents were making sweeping claims for design as a "competitive advantage" as if they had invented it. "[Tim] Brown's 'new' design thinking approach," they wrote, "… is ultimately formulated at a rather low resolution level. The instructions are not empirically nor theoretically supported; they are a generalization of his own experiences packed in a kind of popularized management problem solving approach."[5]

Others expressed similar views. Design expert Brian Ling argued that the oversimplification of design thinking – packaging it "like a Happy Meal" – was killing creativity;[6] the field had been dumbed down to appeal to a business audience and had become the latest business fad. Others argued that design thinking would fail because it was misunderstood and had not been integrated with business thinking.[7]

Yet many felt there was more to design thinking than the latest business fad. We met Donald Norman, user-centred design guru and author of the classic *The Design of Everyday Things*, in chapter 1. He was just as sceptical about design thinking as many others but a little more sanguine. To Norman, design thinking was a myth – but a useful one.[8]

Management scholars weighed in, arguing that, imperfect as the term was, design thinking had something to offer managers. Lucy Kimbell, an associate fellow at the Saïd Business School at the University of Oxford, was also sceptical about the term but argued for a "rethink" that focused more on the practices of different professions in different situations.[9] Fred Collopy of the Weatherhead School of Management had a similar discomfort and, like Kimbell, argued for a shift in focus: "I would suggest that we should focus instead on building and describing an arsenal of methods and techniques, many of them drawn from various extant design practices, that are applicable to the domains and problems in question."[10]

Kimbell's and Collopy's ideas made sense to me – up to a point. For all its imperfections, the term "design thinking" is now well established. For organizations, what matters is not the label but its ability to provide a fresh perspective through its methods and iterative approach.

Design thinking isn't *just* an arsenal of methods, though. It is different from managerial thinking, and not easily picked up by managers. For one thing, the design field has a rich history and knowledge base that take years to learn. For another, its very differences from managerial thinking – such as reflective practice, as well as willingness to suspend judgment and to reframe the problem – make it challenging to apply in business and public-sector organizations.

Yet some organizations have established a strong foothold for design thinking. These organizations have faced tensions of their own in implementing it and have found ways to deal with them.

Four Case Studies in Design Thinking

From Chicago, my research led me to organizations around the world that have been trying to implement design thinking. I interviewed more than thirty organizational designers, design leaders, and experts in large organizations about their initiatives in design thinking, most of which took the form of innovation labs. The organizations included government departments, Fortune 500 companies, and large non-profits in Europe, North America, and Asia.

As much as I could, I paid a visit to the organization to see its physical surroundings and get a sense of its culture. In one case, I ran a three-hour workshop with an internal team of design thinkers to trace the history and challenges in their program; in others, I separately interviewed several designers in the same organization.

I was greeted warmly. My respondents were remarkably open, generous with their time, and often surprisingly frank about the difficulties they faced in their organizations.

Design thinking has captured the imagination of many managers. Around the early 2000s, organizations in the private, public, and non-profit sectors began to experiment with design thinking, an experiment that continues to gather pace around the world.

Storytellers in Design Thinking

To help you find your way through all the stories I discuss in this book, the following is a list of the of the key people I interviewed, along with their affiliations. Some preferred to remain anonymous, and I interviewed many others in the course of my design journey. Their ideas were immensely valuable in shaping my thinking.

The storytellers in this book

NAME	ORGANIZATION	POSITION	LOCATION
Alex Ryan	Alberta CoLab	Senior Systems Design Manager	Edmonton, AB, Canada
Anna Kindler	University of British Columbia	Vice Provost and Associate Vice President, Academic	Vancouver, BC, Canada
Brandon Riddell	Canadian Tire	Manager, Canadian Tire Innovations	Waterloo, ON, Canada
Brian Zubert	Thomson Reuters	Director, Thomson Reuters Labs	Waterloo, ON, Canada
Chris Ferguson	Bridgeable	CEO	Toronto, ON Canada

NAME	ORGANIZATION	POSITION	LOCATION
Christian Bason	MindLab	Director	Copenhagen, Denmark
Cindy Tripp	Procter & Gamble	President, Cindy Tripp & Company	Cincinnati, OH
Craig Haney	Communitech	Head, Corporate Innovation	Waterloo, ON, Canada
Dan Elitzer	IDEO	Blockchain and Digital Identity Lead, IDEO CoLab	San Francisco, CA
David Aycan	IDEO	Managing Director, IDEO Products	San Francisco, CA
Holly O'Driscoll	Procter & Gamble	Global Design Thinking Leader & Innovation Strategist	Cincinnati, OH
Jess Roberts	Allina Health	Principal Design Strategist	Minneapolis-St. Paul, MN
Joe Gerber	IDEO	Managing Director, IDEO CoLab	San Francisco, CA
John Body	Australian Tax Office	Principal and Founder at ThinkPlace	Canberra, Australia
Judy Mellett	TELUS	Director, Service Strategy & Design	Toronto, ON, Canada
Mark Leung	Rotman School of Management	Director, DesignWorks	Toronto, ON, Canada
Markus Grupp	TELUS	Senior Manager, Service Design & Innovation	Toronto, ON, Canada

NAME	ORGANIZATION	POSITION	LOCATION
Mathew Chow	IDEO	Senior Design Lead	San Francisco, CA
Ronna Chisolm	Dossier Creative	Business Strategist, Co-Founder	Vancouver, BC, Canada
Rocky Jain	Manulife	Director, RED Lab	Kitchener, Canada
Thomas Prehn	MindLab	Director	Copenhagen, Denmark
Wendy Mayer	Pfizer	Vice President, Worldwide Innovation	New York, NY
Xavier Debane	Manulife	Vice President, Innovation and Business Development	Toronto, ON, Canada

What these organizations had in common was their recognition that "business as usual" was not working. The world was becoming complex, globalized, and wired. Technology offered mind-bending solutions but created mind-bending problems too. Users had diverse lives and faced diverse challenges; they could communicate instantaneously and widely about their experience. Disruptive innovation was seen as the answer to a disrupted social order. Design thinking seemed to offer innovative solutions to wicked problems.

For most organizations that implemented it, design thinking began as a tentative step into the unknown; over time, some developed internal labs, while others tried to create quasi-independent innovation units. Still others tried to diffuse design thinking across the organization. In some cases, momentum has steadily built over time; in others, design thinking has waxed and waned with changes in leadership.

For all its attractions, design thinking can be an uneasy fit in large organizations. I found that such initiatives live in a persistent state of tension around three issues: their cultural engagement with the organization; how radical their innovations are; and taking on the user's point of view. I call these the *Tension of Inclusion*, the *Tension of Disruption*, and the *Tension of Perspective*, respectively. I will discuss them later in this chapter and take each one in turn in chapters 3, 4, and 5.

The Three Tensions of Design Thinking in Organizations

Design thinkers approach the world with a distinct mindset, methodology, and purpose. It can be challenging to align these with the day-to-day business of organizations, particularly large organizations. I found that design thinkers in organizations face three fundamental tensions:

1 The *Tension of Inclusion*: Distance from the day-to-day pressures and politics in organizations can be a good thing, but too much distance can lead to isolation.
2 The *Tension of Disruption*: Design thinkers can have trouble pursuing disruptive innovations while meeting demands for incremental innovations – a difficulty that increases as the lab becomes better known.
3 The *Tension of Perspective*: Innovations are embedded in complex systems inside and outside the organization; it is difficult to take both a user-centred view and a systems view at the same time.

I've called these concepts "tensions" because they are chronic conditions that design thinkers live with every day. They never go away and are not resolved by one-time decisions – but, as we'll see later, they may be reframed.

Four of the organizations are representative of the issues – and best practices – that I found in organizational design thinking initiatives:

The Australian Tax Office, a tax authority with a diffused design
   thinking program;
Procter & Gamble, a multinational consumer-products
   manufacturer with a comprehensive innovation program;
The Mayo Clinic, a large non-profit hospital with an internal
   design lab; and
MindLab, a quasi-external government innovation lab.

Throughout this book, I will use examples from the organizations I studied to illustrate the tensions I found. I take a deeper dive into these four and return repeatedly to them. I introduce each below and provide some background on their programs.

Designing Thinking in Taxation: The Australian Tax Office

By the late 1990s, after decades of a rigid, punitive approach with taxpayers, the Australian Tax Office (ATO) had earned a reputation as one of the Australian government's most feared and hated agencies. The corporate tax system was seen as complex and Byzantine. Relations with taxpayers and with tax professionals were at a low ebb.

A complex, difficult-to-navigate tax system benefits no one: not the taxpayer, not the collection agency, not the politicians who have to deal with frustrated constituents. Yet it can be horrendously difficult to change processes and systems that have been layered on top of one another over time and are thoroughly interwoven. Added to this were a bias for command and control at the ATO and the risk-averse culture of bureaucracies everywhere.

The ATO's initiative in design thinking grew out of an earlier focus on strategy and visualization. These approaches had greatly advanced the ATO's thinking, yet the assistant commissioner at the time, John Body, and others felt that it was missing the crucial perspective of the taxpayer.

The concept of taxation "design" ushered in a completely new way of working. The ATO hoped to transform its relationship with taxpayers. However, it did not create an identifiable "centre" for design thinking: such a centre would have been difficult to sustain in the face of periodic budget cuts. "We built all these islands of capability through the organization that were stitched together by the brand of 'design,' but they weren't centrally funded," Body told me. "I just knew that if it was a target, it probably wouldn't have a long shelf life." Instead, design was seeded throughout the ATO through conferences and communities of practice.

One early project dealt with corporate tax. At the time, the legislation required a separate tax return for each company within a conglomerate. This created a significant burden for the largest companies, some of which had to prepare separate returns for more than one hundred subsidiaries. Accordingly, the government was considering a change that would allow corporations to file as a single, consolidated unit. The actual *process* of filing a single tax return – not just the return itself – needed to be designed, and the

ATO took this on as a user-centred design challenge. Said Body, "It really was an experiment, where we tried things like prototyping: we actually constructed physical prototypes and walkthroughs, and took tax accountants through those walkthroughs. A lot of visualization, a lot of collaboration … the hallmarks of the design thinking approach." From there, said Body, "progressively, the concept [of design thinking] just took off."

As design took hold over the ensuing years, the ATO worked on hundreds of projects in a wide variety of areas. In spite of this, however, interest in design has waxed and waned. There has been talk of conducting a review, with a view to sharpening the ATO's design capability.

Design Thinking in Consumer Products: Procter & Gamble

In a single day in March 2000, Procter & Gamble's stock dropped more than 30 percent. With its core business in decline and no clear growth strategy, the company was excoriated in the business media and investors were exiting in droves.

To an outsider, a 165-year-old detergent company hardly seems a likely innovation hotbed. Yet, for A.G. Lafley, brought in as CEO in June of that year, innovation was exactly what Procter & Gamble (P&G) needed as its central organizing principle. Cindy Tripp, who later led P&G's Global Design Initiative, told me that while the company was very good at inventing technology, superior products alone often weren't enough. Overall product rating (consumers' evaluation of product performance in tightly controlled tests) was considered to predict marketplace success. But in many cases, said Tripp, "overall product rating started to not correlate with in-market success. Why was that? That was the big dilemma."

Lafley's first major initiative was "Connect & Develop," a program to link up with university labs, suppliers, and even competitors and apply P&G's research and development, marketing, and manufacturing skills to develop ideas into commercial ventures.

Meanwhile, Lafley moved ahead with design thinking. As head of P&G Asia in Japan, he had seen the power of design. According to Tripp, "The mantra became 'consumer response' and 'Let's understand people's needs, and if we understand people's needs, then we can design things and invent things that meet those needs.'" In 2001, Lafley appointed Claudia Kotchka P&G's first vice president for Design Strategy and Innovation.

From the beginning, the goal was to embed design thinking across the organization, starting with the executive team, who travelled to San Francisco for a two-day workshop with design firm IDEO. The workshop showed that design was all about customer experience, not just making things pretty. But how could this shift in thinking shape innovation across a multidivisional organization of more than 100,000 employees?

The design function – or, as it became known, the corporate design capability – was a catalyst. Kotchka founded P&G's design lab, called clay street, in 2004. Housed six blocks from P&G's head offices in a former brewery, clay street was to be both a problem-solving lab and a design thinking training facility.

One of clay street's first projects was to revamp the tired Herbal Essences shampoo brand, then a dark-green product packaged in clear bottles. The team developed a new vision of "organic" products away from old, outdated associations with herbal tea and granola and towards more contemporary connotations of smoothies and brightly coloured blouses. This vision led to modernized opaque bottles in pink and other colours and the tag line "Discover pure botanical bliss."

At clay street, teamwork, creativity, and human potential are articles of faith and are expressed in its own creed:

- We believe in the power of teams – they are more powerful than the sum of their parts
- We believe that people thrive in relationship
- We believe that creativity isn't the domain of chosen few – it is simply part of being human
- We believe in playful spirit
- We believe that genius lies in everyone – it only needs to be revealed[11]

These beliefs are the foundation of "enduring truths" of creative teams and integrative leaders: *intention* to clarify and orient, *compassion* to be fully human, and *connection* to bring people and ideas together. More concretely, these truths translate into nine experiential aspects of the clay street experience:

INTENTION
- Set initial conditions
- Slow down to go fast
- Make the invisible visible

COMPASSION
- Hear all voices
- See with new eyes
- Fall in love

CONNECTION
- Nurture self-discovery
- Jump into ambiguity
- Share stories[12]

Yet with leadership changes, design has ebbed and flowed at P&G too. Kotchka retired in 2004, handing over to Tripp, who retired in 2012. Lafley stepped down in 2009 but returned in 2013 after his successor resigned amid heavy criticism. David Taylor took the reins in 2015, promising to accelerate cost-cutting plans and shake up the corporate culture. In spite of these changes, design thinking has grown: from zero in 2004, the design network grew to 100 facilitators by 2008. By 2012, it was 350.

Design Thinking in Patient Care: The Mayo Clinic Center for Innovation

In the early 2000s, the Mayo Clinic in Rochester, MN, was considering a new approach. In an institution celebrated for its groundbreaking research and its deep commitment to patient care, some senior doctors felt that not enough attention was being given to the delivery of care.

In spite of great progress in drugs, vaccines, treatment, and technology over the centuries, little had changed between patients and physicians. Technological and social changes had put more information and power in patients' hands than ever before, yet treatment facilities were essentially unchanged and the doctor-patient relationship was still paternalistic. The layout, look, and feel of examining rooms had also remained unchanged, as illustrated by the paired images in Figure 2.2, one taken in 1954 and the other in 2012.[13]

In 2002, two senior doctors at Mayo, Dr Nicholas LaRusso and Dr Michael Brennan, launched SPARC – for *See, Plan, Act, Refine, Communicate*. Said Brennan, "We never had something similar [to medical research] that can study the processes by which care is delivered. So we thought, well, why not?"[14]

 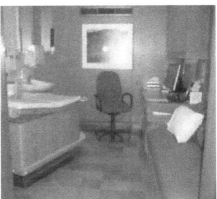

2.2 Exam rooms in 1954 and in 2012
Credit: Used with permission of Mayo Foundation for Medical Education and Research. All rights reserved

Housed in a corridor in the Department of Medicine, SPARC included medical professionals, business strategists, and designers in the hope of fostering close collaboration on innovation in patient care. The initiative was financed by internal funds and philanthropic support. In its first two years, SPARC conducted more than twenty projects. These included redesigning patient exam rooms, developing a check-in kiosk, and developing a new system of education cards for diabetes patients.

Over time, other innovation initiatives were brought in and SPARC evolved into the Center for Innovation (CFI), a fully staffed and funded lab that focused on the design of patient care. Where SPARC had been conducted quietly and behind the scenes, CFI represented a shift to a more public, visible endeavour to improve the delivery of patient care at Mayo.

In one project, Reengineering Dialysis (RED), a kidney-dialysis team mapped the patient's experience with dialysis and developed an integrated-care team approach that took into account medical and non-medical aspects. Palliative care doctors were included; team members were trained in working with patients and families; and, armed with an in-depth understanding of patients, the CFI's designers could develop useful, patient-responsive educational materials.

The RED project had very positive results: hospital admissions and in-hospital dialysis fell; patient, provider, and care-team satisfaction all increased; and there were significant cost savings.

The CFI became a significant – and public – initiative, hosting a large annual conference in health care design that attracts health care practitioners and designers from around the world. Yet the cultural challenge of being embedded in a sceptical "prove-it" culture has continued to dog its efforts.

Designing Thinking in Government Services: MindLab

In the early 2000s, the Danish government was experimenting with design thinking with a unit called MindLab. MindLab was initially about disrupting the bureaucracy – "the equivalent of throwing a grenade" at it, in the words of its founding director, Mikkel B. Rasmussen, then head of Business Affairs in the Ministry of Industry.

MindLab's initial goal was to create the optimal conditions in the ministry for creativity and new ideas. With five full-time employees, it was in no position to disrupt government on its own. However, with skills in facilitation, teambuilding, hosting, and policy development, the MindLab team could exert an influence through creative collaboration within the ministry.

The group hoped to become a catalyst for change at the level of processes, policy development, and organizational development.

The outcomes would include faster reaction times, quicker implementation of ideas, and improved creative competencies within the ministry itself. Its radical interior design, by artists/designers Bosch & Fjord, with mobile furniture, orange pillows, and "The Mind" – a ten-square-metre oval think-tank space with whiteboard walls – signalled that the activities there would be distinct from the day-to-day routine of government.

A project for the National Board of Industrial Injuries explored the experience with the system of those who had suffered industrial injuries. By making videos of interviews with these individuals, MindLab developed a user journey of each person's experience of the handling of his or her entire case. The videos and journeys provided the board with a convincing picture of how the system appeared from the perspective of the user. New ideas were developed by storyboarding different processes and outcomes. As a result of the project, the board made a series of changes in its protocols for dealing with injured persons.

MindLab emphasizes openness and learning (Figure 2.3). Its staff members act as advocates for innovation in the public sector, conducting academic and professional research, publishing articles, and speaking at conferences around the world. Since many of the challenges faced by governments are common across countries, the approach helps MindLab deepen its understanding of systems and how to change them.

Over time, MindLab evolved from its "hand grenade" aspirations to a more strategic approach to systems change. "You can't go out and redesign society," its director, Christian Bason, told me in 2014. "What you can do is work within a complex system to find levers, or even … [like] organizational acupuncture: where are the pressure points you can actually address to make things happen in the direction you want."

2.3 MindLab's home page: http://mind-lab.dk/en/
Used with permission

Bason left MindLab in 2015 to be succeeded by Thomas Prehn. Under Prehn, MindLab has graduated from acupuncture to deep engagement with the bureaucracy and has undertaken projects to bring about behavioural and cultural change and enact a new vision of the public service.

MindLab started small, primarily as a workshop facilitator. However, like the Mayo Clinic, it soon confronted the limitations of this approach. With the full support of senior levels of government, it expanded its activities, first to applying the methods of user-centred design to public services and later to influencing the system at a deeper level.

Each of these organizations, in its own way, dealt with the three tensions of Inclusion, Disruption, and Perspective. Before turning to these tensions, let's take a closer look at why organizations embark on the journey to begin with.

Why Organizations Implement Design Thinking

It may surprise you that design thinking is not just about innovation – and even that sometimes, innovation takes a back seat to other goals. I'll go into these goals in more detail at the end of the book, but for now suffice it to say that there are many ways of implementing design thinking and many reasons for organizations to embark on it. For numerous organizations, innovation *was* an important goal, albeit often not the only one:

ORGANIZATIONS' GOALS IN IMPLEMENTING DESIGN THINKING
Innovation: Facilitating innovation, particularly "disruptive" in-
    novation
Internal change: Changing mindsets, perspectives, and behaviour
User experience: Developing better experiences for customers
Collaboration: Fostering internal teamwork and breaking
    down silos
Talent: Attracting and retaining highly creative people
System change: Bringing about fundamental changes in
    organizational and social systems

The ATO's goal was to become more user-centred: strategic think-ing was helping, but it was felt that the complexity of the tax system was counterproductive. Taxpayers were evading taxes not because they were criminals, but because it was sometimes just too difficult to navigate the system. The ATO's own predatory attitude towards taxpayers was counterproductive, as it fostered a taxpayer culture of "getting away with what you can."

Designers use the term "outside-in" to mean looking at the situation from the point of view of people external to the organization – as opposed to "inside-out," which represents the internal perspective on the problem. At the ATO, the perspective shift to "outside-in" was quite dramatic. A noted academic and consultant, Richard Buchanan, was brought on board to help with the transition to design thinking. Buchanan interviewed about twenty of the ATO's personnel and commented that while everyone talked about the tax system, *individual taxpayers did not experience the whole system – only their pathway through it.*

Up to this point, the ATO had been looking at things strategically – at the system as a whole – rather than on the different impact it was having on different types of taxpayer. As Body told me, "For us ... that was a very profound statement, because it really reframed us from 'We're trying to run this whole thing for the country' to 'Maybe we should be designing pathways for cohorts of people and designing them more carefully and intentionally.'"

The ATO's perspective shift was from thinking of taxpayers in aggregate, impersonal terms – as "taxpaying units," if you will – to seeing them as individuals, or groups of individuals, who faced unique issues of their own. It's a fundamentally different way of looking at problems.

Procter & Gamble's goal, on the other hand, was to deal with intensifying global competition and technological shifts. Having seen the power of design in Japan, Lafley wrote in 2008, "Design was a missing ingredient in our quest to achieve superior organic growth ... I believed the design thinking approach could open up new possibilities for P&G."[15]

2.4 P&G's home away from home, 1340 Clay Street

Lafley's interest was in making the culture of a huge corporate bureaucracy more innovative and nimble in the face of massive changes in its environment. This meant that the design function needed to spread the seeds of design thinking through training and building a large internal network.

To see this in action, I visited P&G's clay street lab in Cincinnati, Ohio (Figure 2.4). Located in a former brewery in Over-the-Rhine, a historic working-class neighbourhood close to the downtown core, it was evidently intended as a "step away" – an escape, even – from the strictures of the corporate head office. The area was a formerly rough but now gentrified part of town, with the occasional syringe still to be found on the pavement outside slick renos of new brick and frosted glass. Inside, the facility was a single room, about twenty metres square, bright, with exposed-brick walls, wood floors, and open ductwork overhead. In the centre was a green carpet with a semicircle of chairs, a flipchart, and a large LCD screen.

My host, Holly O'Driscoll, warmly welcomed me to Cincinnati. O'Driscoll is a global design thinking leader at P&G – an expert facilitator who both helps teams solve pressing problems and spreads the design network by training other facilitators. To my mind, she embodied design thinking at P&G: open, helpful, and positive, she was not afraid to challenge orthodoxy and encouraged teams to do the same. The green carpet, she explained, was a "safe space" where workshop participants could speak their mind without penalty.

I participated in an innovation session with one of the brand teams, a cross-functional group that included representatives from marketing, sales, R&D, and design. Some of the participants had been to a design thinking workshop before: they were thoughtful, curious, and, with O'Driscoll's encouragement, creative. It seemed that within this room at least, design thinking was working. Whether P&G was closer to the across-the-board cultural change envisaged by Lafley, I could not tell – but with the design network steadily expanding, it looked as if progress was being made.

For the Mayo Clinic, healthcare was ripe for disruption, and design thinking promised to provide it. In a 2009 article, CFI associate director Alan Duncan and designer/researcher Margaret Breslin wrote, "It is axiomatic that the US healthcare system almost universally underperforms. Almost no one is satisfied with the current system of delivery and payment of health services. In fact, if the most vocal healthcare quality critics are to be believed, the system we entrust to make us healthier and extend our lives routinely does precisely the opposite."[16]

The CFI's mission, then, is to "transform the experience and delivery of health care." To accomplish this, it focuses on specific "innovation platforms." In its Practice Redesign platform, CFI aims to reduce outpatient costs by 30 percent. The Community Health Transformation platform is based on a "Triple Aim" model of improving population health, enhancing patient experience, and reducing per-capita costs. The Care-at-a-Distance platform aims to develop sustainable models that extend specialty care beyond the traditional hospital/clinic setting, such as underserved areas, affiliated practices, and patients' homes.

Part of the CFI's work is to foster a more innovative culture at Mayo, and for this reason the CFI has a number of outreach programs to connect with sympathizers across the institution. It would be a mistake, however, to think that the CFI is taking on cultural change as its primary goal. Scientific scepticism is deeply rooted in medicine, and the Mayo Clinic is naturally risk averse – as one might expect, indeed hope, in any medical facility. So unlike the P&G experience, significant cultural change is not a realistic aspiration at Mayo.

MindLab, in spite of its early aspirations to start a revolution within the Danish government, came to see itself as an innovation facilitator. Like bureaucracies everywhere, Denmark's government has to contend with multiple constituencies and interests. In such a system, collaboration is key: it is one thing to come up with an innovation, another to implement it on a larger scale. MindLab's motto became "facilitate, don't consult": working as a peer with governmental colleagues meant that it could extend its reach into the implementation of projects and thus have a greater effect.

However, MindLab still feels it has an important role to play in system change: to be the voice of the user in the system and a catalyst for cultural change. Like the ATO, but on a broader scale, it promotes cultural change to help public servants develop a more innovative, "outside-in" perspective.

In one project, MindLab worked with the Ministry of Industry, Business and Financial Affairs to help enact the ministry's strategy of becoming more "agile." While everyone liked the idea of being agile, nobody really knew what it meant in specific terms. Christmas "Advent calendars" were provided to ministry staff; each day in December, civil servants opened a "window" in the calendar to find a micro-behaviour that reflected agility. Said Thomas Prehn, "For all of December, you just have a ministry going completely crazy with agile, and then when December's over, a lot of that disappears, but some of the language will stay behind, and you will also see some of the behaviours stick."

MindLab's facility is more like a boutique design studio than a government office. The space is bright and colourful, the furniture is mobile, and there is an open floor plan (Figure 2.6). At one end, the submarine-like Mind offers an enclosed space for focused thinking (Figures 2.7 and 2.8).

Several projects cut across government agencies, and MindLab's role is to challenge these different parties to take an integrated perspective. Since users do not see the distinction between different silos and expect a cohesive experience, MindLab helps facilitate co-creation in which different ministries participate to find user-centred solutions.

2.5 MindLab's studio in Copenhagen

Each of these organizations had its own reasons for adopting design thinking. While they have stood the test of time, none experienced dramatic, overnight change. Each, however, had to deal with the three tensions of Inclusion, Disruption, and Perspective.

2.6 MindLab's studio in Copenhagen

2.7 The Mind at MindLab

2.8 Inside The Mind

The Three Tensions of Design Thinking in Organizations

As a way to solve problems, design thinking has downsides for large organizations. It may not provide ready answers to the original question, instead questioning the question itself. It can be disruptive; it can consume time and resources with uncertain results. The results themselves are hard to measure. As a result, many attempts to implement it have run up against established organizational systems, cultures, and processes.

Yet in spite of the challenges, organizations like the ATO, P&G, the Mayo Clinic, the Danish government, and many others have met with success. In this and subsequent chapters, I will take a close look at the obstacles these organizations have faced with design thinking and the strategies they have used to overcome them.

Design thinking programs live in tension. To survive and thrive, they manage this tension on a daily basis – not by making stark tradeoffs, but by finding ways of navigating it and even using the tension to their advantage. In my research, I found they had three particular tensions in common: the Tension of Inclusion, the Tension of Disruption, and the Tension of Perspective.

The first tension is *Inclusion:* Every successful design thinking initiative I encountered had what one interviewee termed "air cover": explicit and consistent support from the top of the organization – often, though not always, from the CEO. Yet even with such unequivocal support, innovation can fly in the face of established organizational culture.

Many successful organizations are "doing" machines, built to accomplish clear goals as quickly and in as efficient a manner as possible. While innovation deals with ambiguous and ill-defined problems, ambiguity in the daily business of manufacturing, financing, and human resources can be toxic. Reflection, iteration, and nonlinear thinking may be fine for a design firm or a consultancy but are not helpful and are potentially disastrous if you are trying to run a manufacturing plant or get an aircraft off the ground.

The difference was particularly visible at the Mayo Clinic, where physicians' formal dress and way of addressing patients were designed to put patients at ease, confident that they were in the hands of competent professionals. Design team members at the CFI dressed casually and were less formal. Their demeanour broadcast their difference from the health care teams.

In response, there is a temptation to build walls – physical or virtual – around an innovation program to protect it. Some organizations move their labs to an off-site location, for example. However, the risk is that the innovators will become isolated from the organization – speaking a different language and dressing and behaving differently. Ultimately, this can lead to irrelevance: to survive, innovators need not only the organization's resources but also access to information and moral support from the grassroots, not just from the top.

This is the first tension. Design thinking programs need to maintain independence from the organization while being thoroughly engaged with it. They need to be simultaneously outside *and* inside, top down *and* bottom up.

The second tension is **Disruption**: "Disruptive innovation" has become a buzzword in business and even in the non-profit and public sectors. Disruptive trends in technology, demographics, and social behaviour create the need for products and services that respond to them. Innovation initiatives are often set up with such a response in mind.

Yet establishing a design thinking program does not make disruptive innovation easy. On the one hand, design thinking means revisiting the core assumptions that underpin the organization's offerings; it involves "problem finding" to identify hidden issues that organizations, and even users, are not aware of; it requires a willingness to engage in abstraction – and it takes time.

On the other hand, innovators in any organization need to work within deadlines and budgets that arise from real-world constraints. Many take on "incremental" projects – tweaking current offerings, experimenting with variations on existing ways of doing things – to demonstrate short-term results. The problem is that it's easy for this activity to take over and be derailed by the disruptive innovation they were set up to do. The more successful a program is, the more demands there will be for incremental work.

The ATO did not set up a distinct lab, preferring to "seed" design thinking across the organization. As John Body told me, the original intent of this was to insulate the program from budget cuts, but it had the effect of grounding innovation in the needs of the divisions, which were inherently incremental. In the meantime, senior managers worked on the disruptive task of redesigning the Tax Act itself.

Design thinking programs need to deliver immediate results, even as they undermine the foundations of the organizations that sponsor them. They need to bolster the organization as they question its core assumptions, to be incremental *and* disruptive at the same time.

Another common reason for setting up a design thinking initiative is to bring the user's perspective into the organization: it can be a powerful impulse for the organization to get closer to its users (or customers), which creates a third tension: that of **Perspective**.

Design thinkers develop products and services centred on the experience of the individual user. Innovations, however, have to do more than engage users: they must engage several different systems and consider related products and services, related activities and experiences, as well as the impact on the social system and the environmental system. In addition, the *organizational ecosystem* is tasked with implementation of ideas: technical support, logistics, plant trials, and dealer relationships are all part of this system.

Design thinkers are regularly caught between the perspective of an individual user and that of the system as a whole.

For all its intentions of "throwing a hand grenade at the bureaucracy," MindLab found that many of its ideas fell on fallow ground when it came to implementation. In response, it embedded its facilitators in the implementation process, carrying the ideas forward into the organizational system to be adapted and modified as needed.

In large organizations, to be a design thinker is to live with paradox, cultivate relationships, and conduct subtle negotiations around tricky issues. Design thinkers need to be as cognizant of the organizational system and its workings as they are of the world of products and users, and must be prepared to become involved in the implementation process. They need to be both user-centred *and* system-centred.

My own tension around the term "design thinking" was ultimately resolved by bypassing definitions and focusing on substance. For the organizations I talked to, the three tensions are less easily resolved. They live with them every day, and while there is no single, definitive way to resolve them, the best have developed some practices others can learn from.

PART 2   **THE THREE TENSIONS**

the tension of inclusion

The Importance of Language

Designers and physicians look for different things and measure results differently. Dr Nicholas LaRusso, co-founder of the Mayo Clinic Center for Innovation (CFI), has argued that "the metrics that we use at Mayo are not necessarily the kind that lend themselves to the things that we're trying to do in the Center for Innovation." What may seem a trivial difference in grammar symbolized this divide.

The *Cambridge Dictionary* has two definitions for the word *experiment*:

> [verb (I)] to try something in order to discover what it is like or find out more about it
>
> [noun] a test done in order to learn something or to discover if something works or is true

Between the verb and the noun lies a gulf of misunderstanding. For the designers at Mayo, to *experiment* was a verb, meaning, simply enough, to try something out. It was an informal process in which one or several things might be changed at a time. You might not know what you were looking for, except in general terms. The process, or what was being tested, could change in response to early results; the outcomes were stories, observations, insights.

Grounded in scientific method, physicians tend to think in terms of the noun. Experiments were hypothesis driven and all about the search for absolute truth. You changed one variable at a time and compared "test" with "control" conditions. Your starting point was the null hypothesis that the change had no effect, and you looked for numbers, statistically significant results to reject the null hypothesis.

The difference was about more than language: it was about what counted as truth. While everyone had the same ultimate goal of serving the needs of patients, designers and physicians had different goals, different approaches, and accepted different forms of data.

There were many other differences in dress, demeanour, and conduct that made the designers stand out from the medical staff. One physician noted the difference as follows: "[Designers] dress as creative people; we're [physicians] very conservative in our dress … their physical appearance is more eclectic and creative, and that puts people on edge when they come in; you're almost not complying with the Mayo Clinic dress code."[1]

Differences like these are the tip of the iceberg. The strength of design thinking – its difference from the standard approach to problems – can also be its weakness in many organizational cultures, where difference can generate suspicion. Ultimately, this can lead to cultural isolation. But there are also challenges in being too close to the mainstream: design thinkers risk losing their innovativeness by being assimilated into bureaucratic cultures.

For the design thinkers I spoke with, the Tension of Inclusion is ever present. In the next section, I'll describe the fine line design thinkers walk in organizations: too different, and you risk being shunned or ignored; too similar, and you lose your raison d'être.

Yet organizations are different and ever changing, and there is no "happy medium" that works for everyone all the time.

Challenging as it is, some organizational design thinking programs have found ways of dealing with it – as good design thinkers will, often through trial and error, and even through leveraging their difference from mainstream culture. I'll talk about these strategies for managing and reframing the Tension of Inclusion in the last two sections of this chapter.

Thinking Different

Design thinkers are *supposed* to think differently from the rest of the organization – that's what gives them the ability to come up with fresh ideas. But how different can they really be?

To develop fresh thinking, design thinkers need to be constantly in touch with the world outside their organization. At the same time they need to bring this thinking into the organization, and to do that, they need to be closely connected to it. On the one side is the risk of alienation from the organization; on the other, the risk of assimilation by it.

Design thinkers typically go to great lengths to connect with the outside world and constantly scan their surrounding environment. One way of doing this is through connections with other organizations.

Some, such as Procter & Gamble (P&G) and Pfizer, develop connections with suppliers and even competitors to spark interesting ideas and partnerships. Others join innovation ecosystems: for example, Communitech is an innovation community of more than 1,000 tech companies based in Waterloo, Ontario (Figure 3.1); and design firm IDEO's CoLab facilitates connections between clients

3.1 The Communitech hub in Waterloo, Ontario
Credit: Meghan Thompson for Communitech

from different industries to understand the impact of emerging technologies.

Groups like Communitech and CoLab provide an environment where embryonic ideas can be freely discussed and nurtured. Public-sector organizations, such as MindLab, and non-profits, such as the Mayo Clinic, make use of conferences to meet other innovators who can stimulate their thinking.

Connections such as these are one vital way of rising above the day-to-day pressures of managerial life, of discovering ideas or approaches to problems, and of protecting fledgling ideas. They allow design thinkers to ask interesting questions and to engage in open discussions that might be dismissed as idle fantasy within the confines of their organizations.

Yet there are limits, and design thinkers can easily become alienated from their organization. "They can't be cowboys or cowgirls

Innovation Trailblazer: Craig Haney

I met Craig on a visit to Communitech in Waterloo, Ontario. He's been leading the charge for corporate innovation in Canada for the last five years.

A graduate of the University of Waterloo's Master of Business, Entrepreneurship and Technology program, and formerly a catalyst for innovation at Canadian Tire, he is the energy behind Communitech's Corporate Innovation program. The program links large, non-tech companies into the startup technology ecosystem, helping them become faster and more innovative. Because he works directly with a cross-section of companies at Communitech, our interview reflected his deep understanding of the common issues that arise in innovation across organizations.

and just do whatever the hell they want," Craig Haney, Communitech's director of Corporate Innovation, told me.

Haney began his career at GoodLife Fitness, later founding Personal Edge Training Inc. He used to show up at Communitech "in fitness gear and workout gear, because that was my brand. I was trying to sell the tech companies these ideas of fitness and health."

Today, Haney, still a fit fortysomething, has a nuanced view of innovation labs. On the one hand, he said, you have to "externalize" an innovation team – even if it is physically located within the four walls of the organization, it needs to occupy a different *cultural* space.

3.2 The Mayo Clinic Center for Innovation

That was what I recalled from my research on the Mayo Clinic CFI. Its studio is located in the Gonda Building, at the centre of the Mayo complex. Through the double doors at one end is the Department of Rheumatology. Yet the CFI's studio space spoke volumes about its distinct set of cultural values: informal, bright, and colourful glass-walled meeting rooms provided inviting spaces for thinking and creative work (Figure 3.2). Not what you'd normally expect to see in a hospital – and that was the point. The CFI was a culture within a culture.

On the other hand, Haney told me, you didn't want to be *too* distinctive. "The lab is a product of the organization. It's not going to change the organization. There are compromises. You are not a startup. You're not self-funded. You are funded by the organization."

For a lab to survive, its director has to be self-aware, humble, and cognizant of what the organization needs.

Still, there are risks in being too close to the organization: while you can influence things from within, it can be difficult to stay distinctive when one is surrounded by a dominant culture.

This was a challenge for the service-design team in the Canadian telecom TELUS, one they were happy to discuss when I visited them in Toronto. A group of ten dedicated people from design and business backgrounds, they were passionate about their work and were steadily finding a place for themselves within TELUS. I spent a morning with them, tracing their history and relationship with the company.

Tossing good-humoured banter back and forth and completing each other's sentences, they were fun to be with, a close-knit team who loved working together. Under the leadership of Judy Mellett, director, Service Strategy & Design, the team had succeeded in carving out a place for itself within an organization that had, initially, little understanding of design thinking. By the time we got together, they felt they were on a roll: they had piqued the interest of product teams, run many internal workshops on design thinking, and created a buzz. They credited that to being embedded within TELUS. "We're not off-site," said Markus Grupp, a design leader on the team. "We're very much embedded in the organization. I think part of the reason we've been able to infuse some design thinking throughout the organization is because we're very much physically located here, where other teams are located."

Yet Mellett was more cautious. "For all the momentum that we've built … I think we're still in a fragile state," she piped in. Unlike most of the labs I visited, the team as yet had no physical home and was under constant pressure to show tangible results. "People are talking about it, and there's a buzz, and we've got a funnel of projects," said Mellett, "but the fragility of what we've built is pervasive ... we are still largely influence without any authority."

In spite of TELUS's experience and Haney's assertion that a lab was not going to change the organization, many of the design thinking labs I spoke to were founded with that express purpose: to change the organization's culture from within. The Australian Tax Office (ATO), P&G, and MindLab are three cases in point. As we saw earlier, MindLab's founding director wanted to throw a grenade at bureaucracy. As MindLab matured, it took on projects to bring about cultural and behavioural change within ministries.

Design thinkers have to have one eye looking outside their organization and the other looking inside it. They need to maintain cultural distance – but if they are to have an influence, they need an intimate connection with the organization's culture too. It is a difficult balance to sustain.

Why the Tension of Inclusion Arises

The Tension of Inclusion arises for two principal reasons: first, the pressures of day-to-day business often work against design thinking. Second, the design mindset and approach to problems are distinctly different from those of most large organizations, and this difference can lead to clashes with the mainstream culture. The difference is highlighted when a lab is located away from the main office.

As we saw in chapter 2, design thinking initiatives are about more than innovation and often seek to bring about cultural change at a deeper level. In practice, this cultural shift can be difficult to achieve.

In some cases, such as the ATO, the cultural change sought is to create more empathy for the user. In others, such as P&G, it is to become more innovative and responsive.

In the beginning, P&G worked to build legitimacy for the design approach. Cindy Tripp, formerly director, Global Design Thinking, recalled meeting some early resistance, but "when you demystify design a little bit for people, they understand it's a rigorous process." Some years on, P&G is going beyond just exposing people to design thinking; for Holly O'Driscoll, the challenge now is to build an internal network of believers to create a "mindset shift." In this, she is fighting for attention in the face of the very real pressures of daily business in a consumer-products company.

Global pharmaceutical company Pfizer developed its Dare to Try program in part to build internal innovation capabilities and culture. The program included a major annual conference "to bring in external thinking, try to inspire or motivate people" and be "a demonstration of the culture that Pfizer is looking to support," Wendy Mayer, Pfizer's vice president, Access Strategy, told me.

However, design thinkers face day-to-day pressures that make such cultural change difficult. At Pfizer, the pressure for quarterly earnings drove internal activity and left limited time and money to invest in design activities, according to Mayer. When the benchmark is quarterly results, it can be difficult to devote precious time and resources to innovation activities whose benefits may be visible only in the long term – or perhaps never.

Moreover, the nature of the design thinking approach itself can also lead to challenges in organizations. We saw in chapter 1 how design thinking is suited to wicked problems. Yet the very qualities that make it work for wicked problems – its iterative, open nature – can also alienate design thinkers from the rest of the organization.

The term "wicked problems" certainly resonates with managers, and for good reason. An apparently straightforward innovation project – say, designing a safe car – can have massive implications for cost, pricing, and customer desirability, and even if these

Worldwide Innovation Leader:
Wendy Mayer

Wendy Mayer is vice president, Access Strategy at Pfizer. An MBA and former management consultant, she is responsible for the strategy for Pfizer's innovative business. During her twenty-year career at Pfizer, she has taken on the leadership of innovation teams on a worldwide scale. She has been identified as a "Woman to Watch" in healthcare, she is on the board of advisors at Pulse@MassChallenge, a digital health accelerator, and is a board member for the Association for Women in Science. While she was very forthright in our interview about the challenges of innovating in a large pharmaceutical company, the initiative has brought about some remarkable shifts in thinking and strategy.

challenges are overcome, safety is still a relative term. How safe is "safe enough"? If the design is successful, there may be unintended consequences, such as cannibalizing business from the company's other products or even changing the standards for the entire industry.[2] Issues like these make innovation a wicked problem, in which the biggest dilemma is not finding a solution but deciding what the problem is.

Wicked innovation problems demand an approach that doesn't just solve a given problem, but defines the right problem to solve. Designers would call this problem finding or framing the problem space, and it happens through iteration. A good design team would take a broad look at the safe-car problem, considering not only what a "safe" car is but also fundamentally exploring customer needs, along with technological and market issues, by trying things out, going back to the drawing board, and trying again.

Most organizations work in a completely different way. Different activities, like the parts of a clock, are interdependent and dynamic and must move together in sync. Each part needs certainty about what the others are doing. Ambiguity slows the works down, and iteration can be an exercise in frustration when you have limited time and a need for clarity.

The disconnect leads to impatience from the rest of the organization, manifested in pressure on design thinkers for short-term results. Design thinkers need what Haney termed "air cover" from top management: a deep, public commitment to making design thinking work. Rocky Jain, director, RED Lab, at insurance company Manulife, told me, "If I'm being completely honest, it requires an element of faith from your executive leadership team, and buy-in that this is the right thing, we're doing it for the right reasons, and it's going to take time. And we're willing to put in the energy and the effort so that we give these people enough time to have success."

Location can also be an exacerbating factor. There are good reasons to locate an innovation lab offsite, but doing so comes with a cost.

The Communitech "hub" in Waterloo is a 50,000-square-foot converted tannery, modernized to host a wide variety of innovators: startups, global brands, government agencies, academic institutions, tech incubators, and accelerators. Each client has its own innovation space, not much bigger than an average meeting room, with shared tables and a latte bar close by. As a result – and this is the whole idea – tech startups, media organizations, insurance companies, bankers, and researchers can't help but bump into one another.

Canadian Tire is one of Communitech's larger members. Its lab has three goals: to attract the best talent – to "out-hire" Google and Facebook; to improve its digital infrastructure, and to act as a catalyst for innovation across the entire organization. "[The rest of the company gets] very, very excited when they hear about some of the projects that we're working on," Brandon Riddell, manager, Canadian Tire Innovations, told me.

Being at Communitech not only helps Canadian Tire stay close to the tech community, but also fosters the climate for innovation: "We have what we call a one-hundred-kilometre moat between us and home office," said Riddell. He was told at the outset, "Just go innovate, be creative."

Yet for all the benefits of distance, being located two hours away – if traffic is good – from the mainstream can make it difficult to catalyse innovation across the organization. "It's very, very difficult" said Riddell. "I mean it's all great [for head office staff] to come out here and say, 'Yes. This is wonderful. We should all work this way,' but as soon as [they] go back, a lot of individuals just get sucked right back into the processes and standards that happen at the office." To some, those who work in the Communitech lab are "crazy cowboys" who operate by different rules.

As the Mayo Clinic CFI discovered, of course, cultural distance is not just about physical distance. Although MindLab's and P&G's design labs are physically within walking distance from their head office, their layout and décor speak more of creative space than corporate conformity. This can result in design thinkers being seen as somehow alien and even resented as nonconformists.

As a result of these challenges – the pressure for short-term results, the iterative nature of design thinking, and physical distance – the opposing risks of assimilation and alienation are never far away. Their presence can have a significant impact on design thinking programs.

The Impact of the Tension of Inclusion

Design thinking's survival and organizational influence can depend on how well it deals with the Tension of Inclusion. On the one hand, exclusion from the dominant culture can result in innovation being discounted as a fringe activity. On the other, design thinkers can be overwhelmed by the dominant culture and fail to produce novel ideas. In either case, at risk is not just the program's impact, but its credibility – and ultimately its budget and freedom to operate.

Design thinking's frequent failure in organizations is evident to Jess Roberts. For Roberts, formerly principal design strategist at Allina Health in Minneapolis and now on faculty at the University of Minnesota's College of Design, design thinking is a broken promise.[3] As it is often deployed, he told me in an interview, it provides only incremental improvements and can even be detrimental to the organization.

"Design," said Roberts, "is typically this consultancy model ... that has incredibly little impact on the way organizations actually operate, or [is] an internal consultancy that emerges and grows at the fringe of the organization, where it then remains and struggles."

Many of the organizations I spoke with had encountered this challenge and had to adjust their expectations. MindLab aspired to have a significant impact on the culture of the bureaucracy but found achieving this goal more difficult than anticipated. At its launch in 2002, MindLab consisted of five people and was an "innovation catalyst" – essentially a workshop facilitator. With skills in creative facilitation, teambuilding, hosting, and policy development, the MindLab team hoped to exert an influence through creative collaboration within the ministry, becoming a catalyst for change. The desired outcomes included faster reaction times, shorter time to implement ideas, and improved creative competencies within the ministry itself.

However, by 2006, MindLab had not fundamentally shifted the bureaucratic culture. "Activities were a little bit too superficial, too short to have a deeper impact," former director Christian Bason told me. "[There was] not enough follow up, a lack of user focus; there was some experience over time, but it wasn't systematic." This lack of impact led to a fundamental rethinking of MindLab's mission, first in 2007 and again in 2011, to (in Bason's words) "model the new culture and the new behaviour through our work ... in collaboration with our colleagues."

Under Bason's successor, Thomas Prehn, MindLab has doubled down on its aspiration to change the culture. Said Prehn, "Innovation can, and should, be within the work of ordinary civil servants." These days, MindLab does not stop at modelling behaviour but works regularly with its client ministries on projects to change bureaucratic culture.

Life on the fringe of corporate culture can be precarious, and support from the top is critical. With the enthusiastic support of A.G. Lafley, P&G started out strongly with design thinking. Yet after Lafley's retirement in 2010, and leadership changes following the retirement of Cindy Tripp in 2012, design thinking floundered.

However, serendipity intervened. Lafley returned in 2013, and at an awards event in 2015, gave a speech in which he cited three important aspects of his vision: cognitive science, inclusiveness, and design thinking:

> Design thinking incorporates creative inspiration, modelling and visualization, and a diverse group of people to apply creative and critical thinking to solve complex business opportunities and problems ... If we continue to explore the potential offered by cognitive science, intentional inclusion and design thinking, then I believe there's a lot more ... progress and potential that can be unleashed in our organization.[4]

About the same time, Roger Martin, dean of the Rotman School of Management, ran a series of integrative thinking/design thinking sessions with P&G's executive lead team. In September 2015, *Harvard Business Review* published a special issue with a spotlight on design thinking.[5] At P&G, people saw these events and took notice: design thinking was back.

It was a lucky break for P&G's design thinkers – but the lesson is that design thinking is highly vulnerable to hostile forces in organizations. Top-level support can provide protection, but inevitable leadership changes mean that you cannot rely exclusively on this this kind of support: you need to manage the Tension of Inclusion.

Managing the Tension of Inclusion

Broadly speaking, design thinkers manage the Tension of Inclusion in three ways: through support from the top, by distributing design thinking throughout the organization, and by demonstrating the value of design thinking programs to business units.

Without exception, every organization I interviewed spoke of the first way of managing the Tension of Inclusion – strong top-level support – from the outset. In three of the four central cases in this book – the ATO, P&G, and MindLab – the CEO or senior bureaucrat was instrumental in the founding of the initiative. In the fourth, the Mayo Clinic CFI, the central figure was the chief of medicine or (as one member of the advisory board put it), "Doctor number 1."

Initially, MindLab was the brainchild of a senior bureaucrat, the permanent secretary in the Ministry of Business, who saw the importance of innovation. "[The Permanent Secretary was] quite a radical person ... quite disruptive in the ways he thought about management and leadership," said Bason. "He was also engaged with some business schools ... who were challenging him on, 'if you're preaching innovation to private businesses, how do *you* innovate? How are you investing in innovation for the ministry, and where does innovation live in the ministry?' And it didn't live anywhere."

For most, support from the top was unequivocal and sustained over time. In a few cases, though, it was limited. "My VP, he says, 'I'll give you a year,'" said Judy Mellett of TELUS. By the time I visited, the program had been in operation for four years and internal demand for project work was building significantly.

Top-level support can take you only so far, and as we've seen, is often not sustainable in any case, as leadership inevitably changes. As we saw earlier, a public statement from A.G. Lafley helped rescue the design thinking program at P&G; but this level of public support was not typical. Nor, in Craig Haney's view, was it necessary or helpful: "You do need someone who's accountable and willing to stick their neck out to say, 'This lab is important.' Absolutely, that person needs to most likely be a C-level person ... but she can't continue to drive it moving forward."

For a lab to be sustainable, Haney felt that the key was an "innovation council." "There can be a single person of accountability, but there needs to be a council set up that they are accountable to, like a board of directors in many ways." MindLab eventually established an innovation council in the form of a board consisting of three permanent secretaries and external experts in innovation.

In addition to maintaining top-level support, it is critical to manage the relationship with the rest of the organization at a grassroots level. Thus, the second way to manage the Tension of Inclusion is to distribute design thinking throughout the organization.

Design thinking programs have two basic forms: a centralized "lab," with its own identifiable home and facilities; or a distributed program, in which design thinking is diffused through the organization. Most have elements of both.

With no centralized lab, the ATO is an unusual example of a fully diffused model. However, even here there were elements of centralization: the ATO set up a "sim centre" to test its ideas on users. But for the most part, the ATO's initiative was about developing and supporting talent within departments. At TELUS, there was an identifiable team, but no physical lab. The team worked as a consultant with business units to help develop solutions.

Most others had a physical centre of some sort. However, the importance of the centre varied. For P&G, clay street was one element in a comprehensive and multi-pronged innovation strategy. According to Cindy Tripp, the corporate design thinking team efforts were focused on applying design thinking to cross-divisional, cross-functional projects, but the bulk of design thinking work was located within business units.

Clay street, another innovation process born out of the design organization, was more focused on team development. Said Tripp, "[clay street] is a highly facilitated and designed experience by clay street facilitators, much like a SWAT team, within the corporate design organization. Design thinking largely lives outside the centre."

Like TELUS, some design thinkers saw their role primarily as problem solvers, while others preferred to act as facilitators. Mind-Lab's motto, "Collaborate, don't consult," made it typical of this latter group, and part of its approach was to recruit nice people. In a 2012 article, Bason and Helle Vibeke Carstensen wrote,

The employees have to be different but not too exotic, have to understand the work of a civil servant without thinking like one. And first of all the staff has to be so likeable that their colleagues will want to work with them, even when there are challenges. Recruiting cannot be too thorough or too careful.[6]

I was intrigued by this interplay between top-down and grassroots approaches and sought the opinions of some experts. Mathew Chow is senior design lead at design firm IDEO, specializing in corporate implementation of design thinking. On a bright day in April, I met him at IDEO's San Francisco office, a converted warehouse on the Embarcadero.

For Chow, grassroots "movements" rather than top-down directives were the key to introducing design thinking. You could "prototype" an innovation lab on a small scale, and scale up from there, he told me, "seeding change by setting up a safe space for it to succeed at first … in the organizations [we deal with], there are supporters of change and people who are more scared of it, and doing it in a small modulation helps galvanize and reinforce and articulate what you're trying to do."

The third way design thinking programs manage the Tension of Inclusion is by demonstrating their value to the organization. This raises the question of how you measure the performance of design thinking.

What you measure, of course, depends on what you want to accomplish. If you want the lab to come up with disruptive innovations, you could measure the number of such innovations in new categories or technologies or the number of patents. If your goal, like many of the labs at Communitech, is to connect with tech start-ups, you might measure things such as number of contacts made, projects resulting from those contacts, and how many of these projects were implemented.

Yet for many, cultural change is at least as important as disruptive innovation. Pfizer's Dare to Try program, started in 2014, was also designed to foster a culture of innovation. Pfizer measures cultural change every year through an internal survey. Two key measures on that survey – "Pfizer makes investments in innovation" and "I'm encouraged to take thoughtful risk" – have seen significant increases over the past two years.

Beyond cultural measures, Pfizer also looks at innovation activity. Wendy Mayer gave a few examples: "How many workshops are happening across the organization? How many ideas have been generated from these workshops? How many of the ideas have moved into experimentation? How many of those experiments have scaled up?"

It's one thing to measure cultural change and innovation activity, but measuring *outcomes* is much harder. Innovation labs struggle to do this, and Pfizer is no exception. Innovations may take several years to come to fruition, and the more disruptive they are, the more time they are likely to take. During their development, they may morph and change and be combined with other ideas, so the final product may look very different from the original idea. Mayer finds that an overly strict adherence to financial measures tends to encourage incremental initiatives rather than disruptive ones.

"We didn't want to reinforce [financial outcomes] because everybody is looking on a short timeline when it comes to financials, and that would just paint us into a very incremental space," said Mayer. I will explore other aspects of the incremental/disruptive conundrum in chapter 4, but the issue here is very real: design thinkers need to be measured by different yardsticks from the rest of the organization. To an extent, they are treated as "special," with the inevitable cultural tensions this creates.

Because of this difficulty, I got the sense that a good story may be more important than objective measures, and Cindy Tripp confirmed this idea: "The more you're in the world of imagining what might be … you get disconnected from the realities that the business has to have this kind of internal rate of return. But storytelling helps. It helps bring people along, so they want to problem solve together, because they understand the 'why' behind the idea."

I came away feeling that the key to managing the Tension of Inclusion was engagement. Gaining the support of top management was a necessary prerequisite, but not sufficient for design thinking to survive. More important was the ability of the program to inspire the grassroots of the organization. Ultimately, results are essential – but even more so are compelling stories.

The Tension of Inclusion, Reframed

Managing the Tension of Inclusion is necessary, but does there have to be a tradeoff between being included and being excluded?

Designers are adept at questioning false choices. My former dean at Rotman, Roger Martin, argued that designers, unlike most business managers, reject false tradeoffs and invent new alternatives[7] – reframing, as designers would put it.

In this sense, some organizations have turned their difference from mainstream corporate culture to their advantage and reframed the Tension of Inclusion. I found three approaches to this reframing: by creating an escape from the organizational routine; by treating a lab as a prototype of cultural change; and by connecting with external communities.

First, design thinking can provide freedom to think differently as well as an escape from the routine. For some – though decidedly not all – design thinking's fluid approach is a welcome change of pace. MindLab, P&G, and many other organizations choose to locate their innovation lab away from headquarters and give it a

3.3 Procter & Gamble's safe space

very different "feel" from the rest of the company. Canadian Tire has its one-hundred-kilometre moat.

Architecture and interior design reinforce the sense of escape: at P&G's creative venue, the green carpet (Figure 3.3) is a safe space where participants are invited to step away from conventional restrictions on their thinking: "We call the green carpet 'The Green Carpet of Candour,'" said O'Driscoll. "That helps quite a bit." As we saw earlier, MindLab's submarine-like meeting room, The Mind, has a similar function of a think lab within a think lab. Even within a design firm, IDEO's Palo office has a meeting room modelled on a yurt, to give designers a quiet location to take notes and draw sketches.

At the ATO, with no physical lab, there was no physical escape, but there was nonetheless a defined community. Body organized three internal conferences, the first dealing with design thinking in the context of taxation; the second, prototyping; and the third, design research. Design facilitators were trained and spread like seeds across the organization, and central support was provided through monthly "Community of Practice" sessions, at which internal design experts could share their experiences in applying design.

At these meetings, they could discuss issues in common in implementing design thinking within their business unit; the meetings were held at 7:30 a.m., and, according to Body, were very well attended. In spite of ebbs and flows over the years, design thinking remains an important initiative at the ATO.

Second, some organizations treat design thinking as a prototype of cultural change. By modelling the innovative culture they want and working to build interest across the organization, design thinkers hope the change will catch on.

At the Rotman School of Management in Toronto, DesignWorks provides courses in design thinking for MBA students within a graduate school that has traditionally prioritized finance, strategy, and economics.

Founded by then-dean Roger Martin in 2005, DesignWorks initially occupied a space about a kilometre away from the school, in a renovated Victorian house at 9 Prince Arthur St. Today, the Design-Works studio is situated in the heart of Rotman's slick new building on the University of Toronto campus.

Mark Leung is director of DesignWorks and was a colleague when I was at Rotman. An engineer and MBA graduate from Rotman, he and I lived through the ups and downs of design thinking counterculture in its early years.

DesignWorks was then a fledgling unit that offered one elective (i.e., optional) course and a study tour for a small cadre of enthusiastic students. Faculty at the time were curious but didn't engage. Said Leung, "If I was to speculate: design was not very well defined, its place in a business school being hard to access both intellectually and physically (we were located off-campus)."

"Roger created a bit of an outpost [at 9 Prince Arthur] – so we had air cover," said Leung. "'Out of sight, out of mind' is the term," he added with a wry smile. "That gave us room to experiment and test to see what works and what didn't work." The early period of invisibility allowed DesignWorks to prototype a different educational culture, one in which students were given much more latitude to explore than is allowed by the traditional lecture/case model of business education.

By the time the new Rotman building opened in September 2012, DesignWorks was ready to become part of mainstream MBA education. DesignWorks has gone from being seen as a fringe entity to having an impact on the school. Rotman now attracts students with diverse backgrounds to its MBA program on the strength of DesignWorks and its design thinking programs: "You see nurses, designers, creatives, theatre majors, people who have been on Broadway, people from all walks of life really resonating with the message of design," said Leung.

Although DesignWorks appears to be redefining Rotman's external reputation, within the school's faculty and administration it is still seen as a fringe entity; however, this perception appears to be changing. "Students want it," Leung told me. "Each year, we get a larger and larger cohort demanding this – and a lot of questions on why design is only an elective, if you're signalling to the market that design is a big part of Rotman ... The students are asking, 'Why doesn't [design thinking] show up in other courses?'"

With pressure from students, DesignWorks is steadily moving into the mainstream in spite of the faculty's initial scepticism. Said Leung, "We now have a business design specialization in the MBA, six design courses, and have hired a full-time faculty member." He acknowledged, though, that the process is slow, though it helps that Martin's successor, Tiff Macklem, is supportive. "Change doesn't happen overnight, especially in education. Ultimately, I would say students played a major role in catalyzing the change."

P&G is also using its design initiative to prototype cultural change, and, like the ATO, is building an internal design community. P&G Design is tasked both with helping business units with specific innovations and with changing their culture. Holly O'Driscoll facilitates both – with the ultimate goal of shifting mindsets across the company.

"Last week," said O'Driscoll, "I was leading an immersion … they're trying to shift the mindset and the culture of their specific multifunctional team. So their problem isn't [so much a specific one, as] they realize that they need to start to tell their stories differently and start to think differently about their innovation programming."

There are many initiatives in P&G's multifaceted program, including Connect & Develop (a corporate innovation fund to support innovation initiative) and staff swaps with Google. Along with role modelling and education by people such as O'Driscoll, the sheer aggressiveness of this program has sent a clear signal to the organization about the importance of innovation and the need to develop an appropriate mindset.

The third way design thinkers exploit their difference from mainstream culture is by connecting with an external community. As we saw earlier, several large companies use Communitech to attract talent and develop connections with the startup community.

Others use external links to build credibility outside the organization, which in turn helps boost its reputation internally. MindLab, for example, encourages its staff to publish, travel, and speak at conferences. In addition to internal reputation, this strategy serves other purposes: it opens up the lab to learning from research and the experience of other public-sector labs, and it provides a way to motivate and retain staff.

The exchange of ideas provides MindLab's staff with recognition and inspiration. Said Bason, "It's one way of investing in our staff and making this an attractive, globalized place to work, to be – even though we're in government. Not so many places in government are that attractive or that globalized, at a time when I cannot pay my staff more than anyone else working at similar levels. But they don't leave."

The Mayo Clinic CFI follows a similar strategy of external outreach. Its design director, Lorna Ross, speaks frequently at conferences, and the CFI hosts a major annual conference, *Transform*, that attracts hundreds of design thinkers from across the health care sector to talk about patient-centred innovation.

Throughout my research, I was struck by the openness of the design thinking community. While large organizations are often reluctant to discuss sensitive issues such as innovation and culture, design thinkers were candid and often outspoken about the internal challenges they face.

For public-sector organizations such as MindLab and the ATO, this openness is understandable, as design thinking is seen as a way of opening up government to the citizenry. Innovation in the private sector is typically more secretive; yet organizations in intensely competitive industries – such as P&G, Canadian Tire, and Pfizer – were extremely approachable and happy to discuss their approach to innovation. (Granted, I had to sign a few non-disclosure agreements about specific projects.)

Design thinkers are a naturally open bunch, but in itself this didn't explain their willingness to talk, even self-critically, about their strategy. I put this openness down to the desire to connect with external communities, which has many benefits.

P&G is – on the face of it – hardly the most attractive place for smart, creative millennials to work: a large detergent company located in a small Midwestern city does not hold quite the appeal of a Google or a Facebook. Being open to publicity helps P&G mitigate its disadvantage in attracting talent. It also helps reassure investors who may be concerned about the company's ability to respond to disruptive innovation.

The Tension of Inclusion is a significant challenge for design thinkers in organizations. C-level support is essential, but in time the initiative needs to stand on its own. Part of this – but only part – is delivering results. The other part is learning to work within, and at the same time change, the organization's culture.

MindLab's founder wanted to throw a grenade at bureaucracy, a sentiment that many in both private and public sectors would understand. But while design thinking may be revolutionary for organizations, for most it is a slow revolution – more like lighting a candle than a fuse.

the tension of disruption

Uberization

With grave concern, Captain Kirk holds the wrist of the unconscious crewmember. "His pulse is almost gone," he says breathlessly to Spock. From his belt, Spock produces a small device and waves it over the listless body. He studies the coloured lights on the device. "Severe heart damage; signs of congestion in both lungs; evidence of massive circulatory collapse," he pronounces in a dispassionate monotone.

On 7 September 2016, *Star Trek* turned fifty. Boldly going where no others had gone before, it was escapist fantasy replete with heroes, villains, sexy body suits, and romance. It offered a vision of an enlightened, peaceful future (at least among humans; Klingons were another matter). Like so many, I was a fan.*

Part of the fantasy was technology. Spock's magic device was a tricorder (Figure 4.1), a piece of technology that became a staple of the multiple generations of *Star Trek* on TV and in movies. Of course, it was too good to be true in the 1960s. It still is. But in the world of Fitbit and iWatch, it doesn't seem quite such a stretch.

---

* Though I preferred *Doctor Who*, despite the absence of sexy body suits.

4.1 A Star Trek-style tricorder
Credit: CC BY 2.0 © Mike Seyfang

At least that's what XPrize thinks. XPrize, an organization that sponsors competitions for radical innovation, launched the $10 million Qualcomm Tricorder XPrize for a real-life wireless device that can detect a range of diseases.

Coupled with social media, tricorder technology could allow healthy individuals to team up with other healthy individuals and crowdsource discounts on health insurance. For insurance companies, this idea undermines the very foundation of their business, where risks are pooled and premiums paid by lower-risk customers effectively subsidize the claims of higher-risk individuals.

In tech and innovation circles, this kind seismic change is often called "uberization." Just as Uber's new business model is undermining the taxi industry, insurance may face an existential crisis before too long.

Uberization affects much more than taxis and health insurance: it is pervasive throughout the economy and very real to detergent companies and tax authorities alike. Yet while they are dealing with uberization, organizations also need shorter-term, incremental innovation to keep improving their existing products and services. This is the Tension of Disruption: how do you stay ahead of mega-shocks while staying contemporary and competitive? A difficult challenge for design thinkers, but there is hope: in spite of the tension, some labs are finding ways of being both incremental and disruptive at the same time.

Uberization's Discontents

While uberization threatens traditional businesses, it creates a new playing field for players who operate according to a completely different rule book.

New players such as Oscar Health Insurance have embraced the technology and the data it offers: Oscar partners with a wearable-device company, Misfit, to provide customers with a free pedometer when they sign up for a policy; the pedometer links with Oscar's health app, and by reaching certain goals, customers earn reward points. In return, Oscar gains data and the ability to select the most profitable customers.

Uberization affects other kinds of insurance too. TrueMotion, a software company, offers a smartphone app that can help insurance companies find the most profitable drivers by tracking driving behaviour. Progressive Insurance launched a pilot program with TrueMotion in 2015.[1] The prospect of autonomous cars raises further concerns for the industry: "How does insurance [work] when 30% of the cars are self-driving? What if GM gives its owners car insurance because they drive autonomous cars?" asks Communitech director Craig Haney.

Other industries also worry that obsolescence is just an app away. With the rapid growth of investment in the fintech – financial technology – sector, bankers are being forced to reexamine their assumptions. SoFi was founded in 2011 at Stanford Graduate School of Business by Mike Cagney, a former executive with Wells Fargo, and four fellow graduate students. By using alumni as online mentors, SoFi used the power of communities to support borrowers and could offer student loans at rates considerably lower than the market rate. Since then, it has developed sophisticated algorithms for selecting the most profitable loan prospects and has expanded into mortgages, personal loans, and wealth management.

What makes SoFi unique is its emphasis on building a supportive online community. Borrowers have access to education events, dinners, and happy hours. There is also an entrepreneur program that allows borrowers to defer payments. SoFi also offers free career counselling and advice to its borrowers.

SoFi is by no means the only online lender keeping bankers awake at night; nor is it the only source of uberization in financial services. Bitcoin is another. In a 2016 speech, Ben Broadbent, deputy governor for Monetary Policy, Bank of England, argued that the settlement technology behind digital currencies could reduce the funds deposited in banks and hamper their ability to lend money[2] – thus undermining the fundamental raison d'etre of banks.

If you think that uberization applies only to tradition-bound industries, think again. Your toothbrush can now talk to your smartphone, telling it whether you're brushing too hard, too lightly, or missing areas. Your fridge can tell you to buy milk on the way home from work and can coordinate your busy family's calendars; not far away are recipe suggestions and a shopping list for that dinner party with the Smiths on Saturday night that you forgot about – but your fridge remembered.

Small wonder that many organizations worry about suddenly losing everything through uberization. Because design thinking offers a fresh way of looking at problems, many are turning to it in the hope that it will help them anticipate change and respond before it happens.

Yet design thinkers typically do not have the luxury of focusing exclusively on major change. Organizations have regular needs for tweaks to their existing products or services, and these too demand reframing and a user-centred approach. It is not easy to be both an incremental innovator and a disruptive one. This is the Tension of Disruption.

Why the Tension of Disruption Arises

Disruptive innovation is hard for at least three reasons. Disruption is about tomorrow, but organizations need to focus on today; it can be tough for organizations to attract and retain creative disruptors; and organizational dynamics can squeeze out disruptive ideas.

Planning tomorrow's disruption and running today's business are fundamentally different tasks, and some argue that the two cannot coexist.

Harvard professor Clayton Christensen coined the term "disruptive innovation" in the 1990s, meaning innovations for new market segments not reached by current offerings. An example would be Ryanair, Ireland's discount airline that serves a low-price segment neglected by full-service airlines.*

Christensen, however, argues that companies don't disrupt their own businesses. They can't, because it is not in their interest to chase after segments that their business model is not designed to serve.

Perhaps not surprisingly, many companies don't accept this way of thinking. The refrain "disrupt, or be disrupted" – which, if you believe Christensen, is ill-advised – is everywhere, including in the titles of at least one book[3] and several reports from major consulting firms.[4]

The Mayo Clinic Center for Innovation (CFI) uses design thinking "to revolutionize the experience and delivery of health care by going beyond process analysis and quality improvement."[5] Disruptive innovation, or "transformation" as it's called at Mayo, is at the core of its mission; it hosts an annual conference, *Transform*, which attracts healthcare innovators from around the world.

---

* Interestingly, Uber is not a disruptive innovation for Christensen. In his world, disruptive innovations, such as, say, Ryanair in Europe, start at the low end of the market and move upwards to compete with existing players. Uber, however, competes head-to-head with taxis for the same customer.

Yet the CFI has to cope with many other demands. In the complex, cost-constrained environment of healthcare, there is a massive need for incremental improvements to treat increasing numbers of patients at reduced costs. The RED (reengineering dialysis) project, described in the sidebar, which involved improved practice integration, was such a project. While hardly transformational, these projects are essential in healthcare. Inevitably, much of CFI's energy is devoted to similar incremental improvements.

Success with incremental innovations helps CFI maintain visibility and a solid track record. Nonetheless, disruptive innovation is, by definition, hard to implement and therefore hard to make visible.

Incremental Innovation at the Mayo Clinic: The RED (Reengineering Dialysis) Project

The goal of the RED project was to deliver the best evidence-based care to patients through a team approach. Changes to Medicare in the early 2000s moved reimbursement from a pay-for-performance model to a per-patient lump sum contingent on meeting quality targets. The major implication of this change for Mayo was an enhanced need for better care at lower cost. A team was formed to address this challenge.

By including a CFI designer, the team, which already understood the provider perspective and institutional issues, learned to adopt the point of view of the patient. Through interviewing and observation, the team took a deep dive into the experience of dialysis patients. Some insights rose to the surface:

"Patients don't get vacations." The burden of kidney disease was a full-time preoccupation for patients and their families, day and night, 365 days a year.

Medical and non-medical considerations were interwoven in the
 dialysis experience, but there were gaps between them. For
 many, kidney disease was one of several illnesses they were
 suffering from, while spending three to five hours on dialysis
 every second day brought major challenges to their lives.
The patient-care team was often patients' sole source of
 support – not just medical, but emotional too. Because of this,
 patients were often reluctant to leave the hospital.
Patients and healthcare providers spoke different languages but
 had common goals and intentions.

Eight patient "personas" were developed to demonstrate the
impact of the dialysis experience on the lives of archetypal individuals.

Dr Amy Williams, a nephrologist on the team, spoke of their
insight as follows:

> In the middle of a lot of stress and acute illness, we were ask-
> ing them to make big decisions: do you want dialysis tonight?
> You don't need to do it, but of course if you don't use dialy-
> sis, you'll probably die by tomorrow morning … What kind of
> dialysis do you want? OK, now you're on dialysis, goodbye;
> you can be dismissed from the hospital. Good luck with your
> new life. We realized that this did not set our patients up for
> success in the future.

Noting that in a national survey, two thirds of patients regret-
ted having commenced dialysis, the team framed the problem
as *integrating medical and non-medical components of the
experience.*

> The team mapped the experience and developed an integrated-care-team approach that took into account medical and non-medical aspects. Palliative care doctors were included; team members were trained in working with patients and families; armed with an in-depth understanding of patients, the CFI's designers could develop useful, patient-responsive educational materials.
>
> The results: hospital admissions fell by 40 percent; there were reductions in in-hospital dialysis. Patient satisfaction, provider and care-team satisfaction all increased. Quality standards were met, and there were significant cost savings.

Writing about the CFI in 2015,[6] co-founders Dr Nicholas LaRusso, Barbara Spurrier, and Gianrico Farrugia recognized this dilemma. Transformational innovation, they argued, was an "evolutionary form of innovation." (If that seems like an oxymoron, it neatly captures the tension at the heart of the Tension of Disruption.) While game-changing innovations had their place, "tearing down everything and starting over is not an option in health care," they wrote.

To begin with, disruption means asking probing questions. According to Christian Bason at MindLab, "The most disruptive thing we often do is to challenge, 'What is the framing? What is the understanding of the problem? From where do we know this? And how do we assume that these are the outcomes we can get?' … and 'Why do we assume that this apparently simple solution or approach will actually work for someone?'"

Many organizations have little tolerance for this kind of questioning. As we saw earlier, fundamental questions can be seen as time-wasting and a distraction from the urgent task of responding to challenges.

Second, for many design thinking programs, it has been difficult to attract and retain people who have both the creativity and the organizational knowledge needed for disruption. "We spent a lot on consultants in the early years," said John Body of the Australian Tax Office (ATO). Eventually, the ATO developed its own design capability. Like the ATO, many of the labs I spoke to emphasized training people internally in design facilitation, rather than hiring designers externally to staff the lab.

Some of this is due to organizations' understandable desire to recruit from within. However, there seemed to be some additional reasons not to hire professional designers. First, internal design labs in large, complex organizations are not places where designers can be set free. As Maggie Breslin, one of the founding designers at the Mayo Clinic CFI, put it, "You have to be pretty humble to do this type of work. It's not a place for a more ego-driven designer, because the nature of the work is that you put it out into the world and other people take it and run with it. So if you want it to still be attached to you, this isn't really the right place for you."[7]

In addition, design is not the same as design thinking, and not all designers are design thinkers. Many do not naturally gravitate to the user's point of view, preferring a more art-centred approach. Moreover, to get anything done in large organizations, you need to work in teams, and some designers work better on their own.

Setting up an internal design lab can be a tortuous political process, one that can test the patience of many designers. At TELUS, design was being done, in different ways, by several teams; the Service Design team's presence risked creating confusion and even friction. Said director Judy Mellett, "It was almost like we had to find something to define ourselves and stay away from some of these other hotbeds." For many months, she worked with designer Markus Grupp to think through the sensitive issue of how the team would define itself in relation to the rest of the organization.

Service Design Leader: Judy Mellett

The TELUS Service Design team, led by Mellett, met with me several times. We mapped out a timeline of the team's history and the highs and lows they experienced.

Mellett's background is in business and product/service development at TELUS. She is the founder and leader of the internal Service Design team: formally, director, Service Strategy and Design. With her team, her focus is on design and delivery of customer experiences that build customer loyalty and sustain the TELUS brand. Over time, word has spread about the team, and its work is now in great demand within TELUS.

While the team was clear on its mandate, there were other initiatives in the organization, and positioning itself in relation to these was tricky. After a good deal of back-and-forth, a solution emerged. "Markus looks up and he goes, 'Oh, there's something called *Service Design*,'" said Mellett. "So we start reading up about it and we're '*That's* what we're going to do.'" It was a political process, a far cry from the design work Grupp was trained to do.

The third reason for the Tension of Disruption is organizational dynamics: the self-censorship that comes with organizational life can stifle radical ideas. This can be exacerbated when business is suffering and careers are on shaky ground – the very conditions in which disruptive innovations are most needed. As one interviewee told me, "[New ideas] could ruin their career. It's too risky. They would not go to the meeting, not share their point of view, for fear of it being held against them for a decade or more ... people are afraid to say what they think, afraid of being judged."

The combination of short-term demands, difficulty in appealing to creative people, and organizational inertia can make it very difficult to be disruptive within an organization. The Tension of Disruption, if not dealt with effectively, can threaten a design thinking initiative.

The Impact of the Tension of Disruption

Management thinkers Michael Tushman and Charles O'Reilly III have a ready response for Clayton Christensen. You *can* disrupt your own business, they say – by becoming ambidextrous.[8] An ambidextrous organization is one that manages streams of innovation that are both evolutionary (i.e., incremental) and revolutionary (disruptive). That sounds easier than it actually is.

Design thinkers deal with the Tension of Disruption every day. Procter & Gamble's Holly O'Driscoll told me, "Absolutely, it's a tension for us and I think for many other players in this space. It's becoming increasingly important to live with that tension because picking one over the other [i.e., incremental over disruptive] are both, I believe, ... wrong answers. It has to be a mix."

All the organizations I talked to had come up with some way of working with this mix. Yet it was a persistent shadow in the background. On the one hand, tack too far towards incremental innovation and you lose focus on the raison d'être of design thinking; on the other hand, too many disruptive projects can bring pressure for short-term results.

The pressures were not equal, though: most of the design thinkers I spoke to were worried about doing too much incremental innovation, not too much disruptive innovation. In some cases, they would start out with disruptive ideas, but these would change over time and end up incremental.

Wendy Mayer at Pfizer seemed to be finding a balance of sorts between these pressures. To begin with, Pfizer's innovation strategy was to find disruptive opportunities in health care: "The initial team was created … to develop new potential revenue opportunities coming from emerging spaces related to Pfizer's business that the executive team and the strategy team were identifying," said Mayer. "So, in the first few years … the team solely focused on scoping out and developing how Pfizer could play a role in defined areas of innovation."

However, by the time she was brought in to head up Pfizer's Corporate Innovation Group, Mayer found that the group was having limited impact. "It seemed that the innovation team was spending a lot of time herding cats across the organization. Most of the effort was around [organizational] structure and scope of responsibility, and less about demonstrating what [design thinking] could potentially offer."

Mayer felt strongly that innovation at Pfizer needed to become more adventurous. Over time, she worked to build a more significant innovation capability, and saw some success. Yet, as we saw earlier, the drive for short-term results is never far from view. "The biggest barrier, I think, is quarterly earnings, because it just drives so much of the internal activity and prevents people from having time and money to invest," she told me.

At TELUS, the Service Design team established itself as an internal consultancy for product groups. In the early days, it had to seek out work: "The early days were very much meeting with as many folks, and coffees, and just chatting around, 'Oh, you have this customer/business problem. Here's how we could possibly help you,' and trying to see if there's actually a problem that we could help teams solve," said Markus Grupp.

Yet, like Pfizer, the TELUS team struggled with short-term thinking. Too often, the team was tasked with finding a quick answer, leaving disruptive opportunities on the table.

Launch timing drove everything, and the Service Design team's frustration was palpable. "What happens – what too often happens – … is [the product group says], 'We spent a year, year and a half working on this. It has to launch in six months. … Please come help me,'" said one of the designers, to some sardonic laughter from other team members. Added Judy Mellett, "I wish more projects would come to us where it's 'Help us define the problem, and *then* help us take this product, a solution that we've identified, and bring it to market.'"

But what starts out as a disruptive project can easily end up incremental. As a project works its way through the implementation process, it is often tweaked, shaped, and moulded to fit the organization's capabilities or preferences. Users may not be consulted about these implementation-phase changes, and the result can be quite different from the original intention.

For one design thinker in a large non-profit company, a bias for "newness" seemed to complicate things: "I think the types of projects we're working on are *too* big … You can come up with an idea and … it will be a lot more successful if you're proposing a new thing. But if you're proposing a *destructive* innovation where you're actually *subtracting* things, it's instantly the exact opposite reaction." Here too the frustration was palpable: "By the time it evolves, and there's been so much input and consensus, you start to see that you're ending up proposing an additional thing, rather than being able to disrupt."

For most, the Tension of Disruption had a definite bias towards incremental innovation. Where design thinking could take root, it tended to lean towards short-term, incremental opportunities. Perhaps Christensen had a point: organizations do not naturally disrupt themselves. Was Tushman and O'Reilly's ambiguous organization one of those nice ideas in theory that proves impossible in practice?

Managing the Tension of Disruption

As we saw in chapter 3, innovation is notoriously hard to measure, and disruptive innovation even more so. Traditional measures, such as number of patents, don't work for non-technical innovations (such as services). Financial measures, such as return on innovation investment (ROII), don't usually shed much light on the reasons for success or failure. Then there's the issue of whether your goal is financial outcomes, customer value, internal processes, or organizational culture;[9] the companies I spoke to were concerned with all of these aspects but in varying degrees.

There is a vast literature on measuring innovation, which is another way of saying that the best minds are still scratching their heads over it. In the meantime, companies muddle through.

Without clear measures, design thinkers face pointed questions about how they are spending their time and money. Because disruptive innovations are harder to measure than incremental innovation, the pressure can be intense.

One response – not necessarily one I'd recommend – is to hide.

In March 2014, the General Accounting Office (GAO) in the United States published a report[10] on the Office of Personnel Management's innovation lab, LAB.OPM. It traced the lab's history – like many, it got its start with incremental projects – and noted that it had plans for large-scale, multi-stakeholder (i.e., disruptive) projects. The report, however, was headlined:

Agency Needs to Improve Outcome Measures to Demonstrate the Value of Its Innovation Lab.

The GAO report was duly reported in the *Washington Post*.[11] The takeaway: "These guys are spending taxpayer money and they can't document the results," as one of my public-sector interviewees put it.

You may not be aware that the Office of Personnel Management (OPM) has an innovation lab. To survive the intense scrutiny of the media, the OPM lab decided to keep its activities below the radar and maintained a low public profile.

Staying out of the hostile glare of taxpayer scrutiny may ensure short-term survival. It doesn't do much to further the cause of disruptive innovation – in the short run at least – nor to change the culture of the bureaucracy.

Happily, there are better approaches than hiding. One is to use models to show the organization how disruptive innovation can be blended with incremental innovation. Another is to play the long game by establishing the lab's credibility through early wins. (Perhaps this is what the OPM lab believes it is doing.)

Classic models like McKinsey's Three Horizons of Growth[12] help put innovation in perspective. According to the model, by improving the performance of core businesses in the short term, and by looking for emerging opportunities in the medium term, and for more speculative ventures in the longer term, companies can balance disruptive and incremental innovation. Shown in Figure 4.2, it's a well-known framework, a favourite of consultants, and several of those I interviewed referred to it as a way of managing their portfolio.

Manulife uses a similar model, the Innovation Ambition Matrix.[13] "You would be familiar with the ambition matrix, maybe, that kind of defines core, adjacent, and transformational innovation" said Xavier

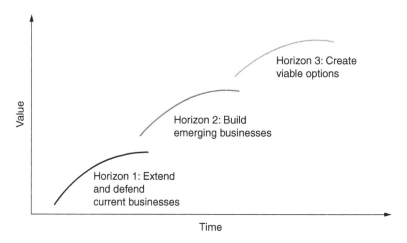

4.2 McKinsey's Three Horizons of Growth

Credit: McKinsey & Company, www.mckinsey.com. Copyright © 2017. All rights reserved. Reprinted by permission

Debane, Manulife's vice president of Innovation and Business Development. (To my embarrassment, I wasn't at the time but read about it later.) "We're using a number of those tools that help us define the extent of innovation, the magnitude of innovation, and where we put our innovation efforts relative to the initiatives we have."

Another commonly used model is the Ten Types of Innovation[14] from Doblin Inc. This model helps innovators explore alternative ways of creating and delivering value to users by considering different points along a chain of value. The punchline is that most companies innovate by focusing on product performance, leaving opportunities in areas like business model, customer financing, and branding on the table. In effect, it's a caution against chasing after disruptive technology when the most interesting, and disruptive, innovations may be under your nose.[15]

At Communitech, Craig Haney suggested that models like these were a way of gaining credibility for the initiative and giving it a sense of direction. "The Three Horizon model really works well, but [sometimes] the Ten Types of Innovation, and maybe the Lean Startup … is a wonderful way to show executives the value of the build, test, and learn philosophy of 'We're not here to fail. We're here to build, we're here to test, and we're here to learn from that.'"

Measurement is clearly a pain point for design thinkers in organizations, and there is no easy answer. I'll return to this topic in chapter 7 with some (admittedly imperfect) suggestions.

Of course, models are great, but demonstrated success is even better. Some design thinkers saw great value in early wins. Certainly, early wins help build a case for the design initiative, but usually these are of an incremental nature: disruptive innovations take longer. Essentially, early wins buy time.

At Rotman, Mark Leung has been buying time for some years now. Leung acknowledges that disruptive innovation in higher education is a slow process, but feels that things are changing.

For students, design thinking is "an easy win in that it's a different pedagogy. [Compared with] sitting in the room listening to the sage onstage, listening to hundreds of sages onstage, and not really engaging with the content … I think the studio pedagogy has been transformational, especially in business education. You're exploring, you're reflecting, you're failing. The fact that there's no right answer, I think that has been very powerful for our students."

It helps that studio learning is already well established in design and other fields, so the early win here comes from adapting it to business education. It has helped build a wellspring of demand from students, who are pushing the faculty to respond.

Yet time can run out on early wins, and sometimes there is a need for dramatic action. MindLab's former director, Christian Bason was recruited after the lab had been in place for six years. The lab was judged a success because it had a broad reach and had established a distinct project-based approach in the Ministry of Business – but it needed to have a deeper impact on the system.

As we saw earlier, Bason launched the second generation of MindLab in 2007, building in user focus and working to change the system at a broader level. User-centred system change doesn't come easy, though, and MindLab reinvented itself again in 2011. In 2015, under its new director, Thomas Prehn, MindLab began to burrow deeper into the system, working closely with ministries to promote cultural change.

Models were good for exposing opportunities for disruption and for linking short-term programs with more disruptive ones. Early wins provided concrete evidence that design thinking could work. Together, these can help reduce the pressure towards incremental innovation. Still, design thinkers are nothing if not ingenious, and I was curious to see how they were thinking differently about the Tension of Disruption.

The Tension of Disruption, Reframed

Could the Tension of Disruption be reframed and companies disrupt themselves? The question goes to the heart of Clayton Christensen's theory of disruptive innovation.

I mentioned earlier that many organizations didn't seem to accept Christensen's ideas, and in any case, the theory itself has come under fire. Writing in the *New Yorker* in 2014, Jill Lepore offered a thoughtful and scathing critique of Christensen's theory of disruption.[16] Some academics weighed in too.[17] Part of the concern was that since Christensen's cases were selected on the basis of market performance, the theory wasn't much use when it came to predicting what would be disruptive and what would not.

I found that some design thinkers were reframing the Tension of Disruption by creating two types of platform: technological and collaborative.

We met Brandon Riddell of Canadian Tire in chapter 3. One of his key goals, you'll recall from my interview with him, was to show the rest of the organization what new, cutting-edge ideas the lab could come up with.

Great, I thought. So if "cutting-edge ideas" were disruptive innovation, just what was he working on? "Christmas lights," he told me. "Mmm ... cool," I said a little hesitantly, wondering exactly what could be cutting edge about Christmas lights. But, Riddell continued, these were not just any Christmas lights: in trade jargon, these were IoT (Internet of Things) Christmas lights that you could control from your office, your car, or wherever.

I was still a bit disappointed. Cutting-edge Christmas lights didn't have quite the same cachet as Spock's tricorder. Riddell went on. "We built out our platform on the back end that will support any ... connected device. Then we've made decisions on the type of chipsets, and then we're passing this information down to all the different business units and saying, 'This is how you approach your vendor. This is the type of information that you can give them if they want to integrate with us.'"

In other words, the Christmas lights were not just a single-shot technology. Riddell's group was using Christmas lights to develop the specs for all IoT innovations as a platform for future products. He was using an incremental innovation to lay the foundation for future innovations – disrupting at a more fundamental level.

"If we have this infrastructure in the back end that we've built out to support it," he continued, "then building one more connected device is ... you know, we do a prototype in a week, versus before it would take us months to do it. What we've done is taken a step back, built out what we need, so that we can move faster in the future."

Now that *was* cool.

In short, Canadian Tire was using technological platforms to bridge incremental and disruptive innovation: "[Canadian Tire is] building technology to actually *extend the digital infrastructure*. They do that by building proof of concepts and then minimum viable products that ultimately will hopefully become real products out in the real world," said Communitech's Craig Haney.

Pfizer had a similar approach but implemented it differently, by funding "use cases" at the business unit level and helping scale them up. Wendy Mayer described how it worked. "So a new technology coming out of Israel: we'll identify a team that we think could be a reasonable use case, but we'll pay for the pilot or experiment. And then, once that's over … the businesses then have to take that on, to scale it more broadly."

The second way design thinkers were reframing the Tension of Disruption was by creating collaborative platforms to forge new kinds of relationships.

In 2002, in the early days of its revamped innovation program, Procter & Gamble (P&G) announced an agreement with its competitor, Clorox, to form a joint venture in the food wrap business, combining Clorox's well-known Glad bags and wraps with P&G's Impress food wrap. The arrangement showed a willingness to think differently about what was otherwise a competitive relationship. This was part of Lafley's Connect & Develop strategy – to build external relationships and networks. The deal was sealed with a formal agreement, announced in the media.

Pfizer has also expanded beyond an internal design lab to engage other companies, even competitors, in collaborative innovation. "What if, instead of thinking about Merck as a competitor, we thought about them as a partner?" asked Wendy Mayer. In a field such as lung cancer, subjects for clinical studies were scarce and difficult to recruit; companies competed fiercely for them.

However, said Mayer, partnerships were emerging. The National Institutes of Health (NIH) was working with a number of different pharmaceutical companies to recruit patients with lung cancer and place them in whichever study was most appropriate for them. "So it's like a mass united recruiting effort and then a collaboration in terms of working across all of the studies, to enable all of the studies to be completed and fully recruited," she told me.

In effect, the NIH was coordinating a different kind of platform: an innovation ecosystem. Just as Amazon is a vending platform where a variety of companies share infrastructure, design thinkers are creating collaborative platforms where innovators come together to share facilities and work on ideas. Communitech is one; IDEO's CoLab is another.

CoLab links companies across boundaries of industry and scale. Joe Gerber is its managing director. Before our interview, I checked out his profile on IDEO's website:

I'm the MBA who's skeptical of business people.

I liked him already.

Gerber was joined by Dan Elitzer, Blockchain and Digital Identity Lead (Blockchain is the technology underlying Bitcoin). "CoLab is kind of a shared lab," Gerber told me. "We're splitting the risk across multiple stakeholders. IDEO is one of them. We're not doing it on a consulting basis; we're actually partnering with each of the members."

I'll admit that if Bitcoin was, to me, the fuzziest of concepts, Blockchain was no clearer. But you didn't need to be a techie to understand what this was: a neat way of bringing inventors together. I was intrigued.

The idea was born of some frustration on IDEO's part. "One motivator was, after years of consulting, being tired of us not making an impact when we thought we could," Gerber told me.

Another motivation was that incremental and disruptive innovations did not live well together. Companies would talk the disruptive innovation talk but lacked the ability or will to walk the walk. "Often our clients come to us asking for revolutionary innovation when they really either want, or are prepared to do, incremental ... innovation," said Gerber. "And so we wanted to create a place for revolutionary stuff, where we were supposed to be taking more risk."

What particularly caught my attention was that IDEO felt that design thinking needed to move upstream into earlier stages of technology research. CoLab was created as a way for innovators large and small to get together, connect, and share risk. IDEO shares ownership of the lab and its discoveries with the members.

"We have different ways to engage our members," continued Gerber. "There's a strategy council that helps set the research agenda and the strategy for the lab itself. On a project-by-project basis, we try to get people from the member organizations to participate on a day-to-day and a week-to-week basis in terms of helping shape the brief, answer questions, make connections inside our organization, show up at workshops ... etc."

In CoLab's original conception, members were chosen to represent different skills and points along the value chain. "We try to make them complementary," said Gerber. "For example, Citi Ventures is one of our partners. We're not going to pull in Barclays or Bank of America or JPMorgan, because we've got that role covered. There are multiple financial services companies, but they play different roles." A second membership tier, in which competing companies could participate, was introduced later.

A good deal of the innovation work was done by temporary fellows and residents. Initially, these were students from Harvard and MIT and, as CoLab matured, more graduate students and professionals were brought in through events such as make-a-thons and three-month residencies. "In the rare case that those projects continue, they [the students] can have that option [of continuing]. Otherwise, they go back to anything else that they're interested in, and they'll have had a three-month intensive learning experience about entrepreneurship."

As you might expect, it was not easy to coordinate all these different members, with different interests, different cultures, and different ideas about what was acceptable risk. For this reason, CoLab was kept small. "We want the interactions to be more meaningful, and we want everybody to know everybody who's participating and build trust. But even so, that's definitely something that's been difficult."

Because companies have diverse philosophies and methods, innovation ecosystems like Communitech and CoLab are in many ways works in progress. IDEO's CoLab is explicitly about extending the application of design thinking, but the companies I interviewed at Communitech were not all wedded to design thinking. Brian Zubert, director of Thomson Reuters Labs, for example, while familiar with design thinking, preferred "big data" analytics as an innovation method.

By creating platforms for technology and platforms for collaboration, organizational design thinkers were reframing the Tension of Disruption. Reframing, however, means being less concerned with intellectual property (IP) and more prepared to share ideas. At Pfizor, Wendy Mayer captured this shift in an industry traditionally obsessed with IP: "[Before,] everything was, 'I have to own it all, and it's all about the IP, and I don't want to work with anybody because there could be some concern that we don't get all the credit or that they learn something that we already know.' All that has changed." Disruption was as much about mindset as method, and collaboration could put innovation into hyperdrive. Captain Kirk would have approved.

the tension of perspective

Seeing from the Outside In

It was a bright winter's morning. Through gothic windows, the sun streamed into the University of Toronto seminar room, casting a warm golden glow. Forty-two doctors and nurses from a large hospital trained sceptical eyes on me. They were there to learn about patient experience; no doubt some wondered what design thinking had to do with them, or what I could teach them about patients.

Taking a deep breath, I opened the session by drawing a line on the chalkboard to represent a patient's journey through medical care. I asked the group to describe what happened on this journey. From their expressions, the question was evidently a bit confusing, but it was early in the day, so they cut me a little slack. The discussion that followed was revealing.

The group comprised teams from different areas of the hospital, and there was little consensus about where the journey began and ended. For most, it began when the patient entered their department – be it Emergency, Radiology, Surgery – and ended when she left. For a few, it began when she entered the doors of the hospital and ended when she walked – or was wheeled – out.

You could see how this made sense: from the teams' perspective, the only thing that mattered was providing the best possible treatment to the patient who came through their door. Yet from the patient's perspective, medical treatment was a long journey that typically began with a visit to a family physician and ended – hopefully – in recovery.

This difference mattered. In the *New York Times*, Dr Danielle Ofri wrote of a profound insight about a middle-aged patient with diabetes.[1] Shocked to find his blood sugar dangerously high, she was even more shocked to find that he was quite aware of his diabetes and the need to control blood sugar. But it wasn't his priority at that time. She wrote: "For my patient, his wide-angle lens took in the whole of his life, of which diabetes was one small part. For me, in the 20 minutes allotted, my lens was narrowly focused on the disease that posed the gravest and most immediate risk to his health." For Dr Ofri, the problem was getting her patient's blood sugar down – as soon as possible. But her patient saw the problem differently: as a taxi driver, he lived on fast food and had little opportunity to exercise. He realized the importance of controlling his blood sugar but he had many other issues to deal with.

It was a perfect example of the difference between an "inside-out" perspective – that of the professional and the institution looking outwards at the patient – and the patient's "outside-in" viewpoint towards the health care system. To Dr Ofri's credit, she realized that without taking the patient's perspective into consideration, she would have no hope of treating this individual. She took the time to work out a plan in consultation with her patient.

Most organizations, not just health care organizations, gravitate towards an inside-out perspective, and a common goal of design programs is to bring in an outsider's (i.e., user's) viewpoint. The challenge is that organizations don't work that way: in complex organizations, you need an inside-out perspective to get anything done. Critical and powerful constituencies can enable, or block, implementation of the solutions design thinkers come up with.

This is the third tension, the Tension of Perspective: while design thinkers tend to emphasize the user's perspective, other perspectives must be considered too. The most common symptom of the Tension of Perspective is failure to implement the ideas that come out of design programs. In this chapter, I'll discuss this tension and how some design thinkers are reframing it.

What's So Bad about Being User-Centred?

While users are important, it is difficult to sustain a user-centred perspective for very long. In addition, the user's view is not the only view. All organizations need to engage an internal implementation system to make projects happen; there are significant stakeholders to consider outside the organization too.

Empathy is a quality we associate with health care workers, and for good reason. To a much greater degree than managers or bureaucrats, empathy is their *job*. We expect them to understand our pain and help do something about it – and if they can't fix the problem, at least appreciate what we are going through. For the most part, they do this very well.

Designers also practise empathy, but in a different way. For designers, empathy is understanding the user's experience of a product or service: what it means to him or her; what feelings it creates; how it affects, or is affected by, relationships with others' where it fits in his or her life; what challenges (pain points) arise. This is a much broader form of empathy than that practised in health care, one that is rooted in the philosophical traditions of phenomenology.[2]

Designer empathy is critical not just in healthcare but in any situation in which users are important. In chapter 2, we saw the dramatic effect of such a shift in perspective at the Australian Tax Office (ATO) when the team began to see the world from the point of view of the taxpayer. I've seen such a shift many times in organizations.

It seems obvious that doctors should see the patient's point of view, that business executives should see things from the perspective of customers, or that governments should empathize with citizens' experience. Heaven knows, they have been told often enough by management gurus. Yet they rarely do. In many cases, they have little direct contact with users; if they do, users are seen – usually benevolently – as outsiders.

This is perfectly understandable. Organizational life is complex. Internal teams tend to focus on managing this complexity, and it is easy to lose sight of its ultimate beneficiaries. A "battlefield" mentality can set in, in which the relationships that matter are those with your colleagues, not with the end users. These factors make designer empathy difficult for organizations to sustain for any length of time.

It's like the well-known optical illusion of the old and young woman (Figure 5.1): when you know about the illusion, you can flip back and forth from seeing the old woman to seeing the young woman, but you can't see the two at the same time. In the same way, you can't be simultaneously inside-out and outside-in.

Indeed, being outside-in can take you only so far. Products and services are a compromise between the interests of users and those of organizations, and the internal perspective is just as legitimate as that of the user. In hospitals, little gets done without the consent of medical staff: just ask those who have tried to introduce dispensers for hand cleaning. Writing in the *New England Journal of Medicine*, Atul Gawande described how staff resistance to alcohol dispensers impeded their adoption:

5.1 Old/young woman optical illusion*

It took ... more than a year to get our staff to accept the 60 percent alcohol gel we have recently adopted. Its introduction was first blocked because of the staff's fears that it would produce noxious building air. (It didn't.) Next came worries that, despite evidence to the contrary, it would be more irritating to the skin. So a product with aloe was brought in. People complained about the smell. So the aloe was taken out. Then some of the staff refused to use the gel after rumors spread that it would reduce fertility. The rumors died only after the infection-control unit circulated evidence that the alcohol is not systemically absorbed and a hospital fertility specialist endorsed the use of the gel.[3]

Not only is the user's perspective incomplete: if it's your only perspective, it may even be irresponsible. The cars we drive have been fitted out for our comfort, not for the good of the environment. Resource development in rural communities allows us to build great cities, while destroying traditional ways of life. Society as a whole has a stake in the design of education – you can't focus just on students, but need to consider teachers, parents, taxpayers, and a host of political and commercial interests.

For design thinkers in organizations, the Tension of Perspective represents a significant challenge. Inside-out organizations ignore the user at their peril. Yet in representing the user's perspective in

---

*   Usually attributed to cartoonist W.E. Hill, who published it in the American magazine *Puck* (1915). The image was probably derived from an earlier German postcard. Other illusions, such as the rabbit/duck illusion, have a similar effect.

the organization, you can to be *too* outside-in. If the perspective of key internal and external stakeholders is not taken on board, the best user-centred innovations may never see the light of day – or will have little impact if they do.

Why the Tension of Perspective Arises

The Tension of Perspective arises from the wicked complexity of large organizations. Because of this complexity, they are wickedly difficult to lead, and effective leaders are rare.

We encountered "wicked" problems in chapter 2: those problems where the biggest issue is deciding what the problem is. Large organizations are wicked problems: complex environments with multiple – often competing – stakeholders, overlapping systems, and a great deal of ambiguity. User-centred design is not easy in such an environment, particularly because it is not always clear that end users are more important than internal "users" of the innovation. Getting anything accomplished requires exceptional leadership to reconcile the competing perspectives; yet this is often lacking.

MindLab's Christian Bason told me that the complexity of government was a wicked problem in itself: "You have the complexity and the wickedness of the problems out in society, and you have the complexity and the wickedness of the systems we've designed … Those systems have legacies that go back to the 18th century; and they have sediments and layer upon layer upon layer of regulation, of procedure, of ways of doing things. Combined with digital and social media and modern ideas of governance, that whole mix … that's a huge complexity in itself."

While government is an extreme example, organizational complexity is not in short supply at large private-sector organizations. Chris Ferguson is founder and CEO of Bridgeable (Figure 5.2), a

5.2 Bridgeable at work
Images supplied by Bridgeable

Toronto design thinking consultancy. At six feet, five inches tall, he's a friendly giant with an infectious passion for design. From his wide experience with Fortune 500 clients in health care, financial services, and telecommunications, as well as in the public sector, he is acutely aware the difficulty in implementing innovation.

Over dinner in Victoria, British Columbia, we spoke about some of the challenges he had encountered. "One thing I've seen," he told me, "is [that] everyone is trying to work towards more of a matrix model, and I definitely think that most, maybe all organizations, we've seen are really struggling." Matrix organization was seen as a way to integrate operations, but organizations had great difficulty breaking away from silos. "The silos don't align with the realities of their customer. Although the realities of the customer don't align with the functions that need to be done." He shook his head and chuckled, a little sadly. "It's kind of this 'chicken and egg' thing. I don't see anybody really doing it well."

Second, the sheer number of different parties involved could make implementing innovation a daunting prospect: "You get these very large amounts of stakeholders being involved in decision making" Ferguson continued. "So you get twelve different functions at the table. Like … any project we do with TELUS or Genentech will have twelve groups, eighteen different groups involved."

This resonated with me. For some time, something had been bothering me about my interview with John Body at the ATO, when he related the "aha!" moment when Richard Buchanan commented that individual taxpayers don't see the "tax system," just their own pathway through it.

I couldn't deny the truth of this. Yes, the individual taxpayer mattered. But surely this was swinging the pendulum too far. Of course the ATO needed to consider users … but there *was* a tax system, and the system made a good experience – or a bad one – possible. That system included the ATO organization itself, its structures,

Service Design Evangelist: Chris Ferguson

Ferguson is a leading figure in design thinking, with a focus on service and experience design. His award-winning design company, Bridgeable, delivers projects to corporate, NGO, and government clients. He shares his passion wherever he can: through teaching in business schools and the University of Toronto Law School, by co-founding Service Design Canada, by serving on advisory boards, and through articles, reports, books, and presentations. His enthusiasm for design is infectious.

He has seen design initiatives succeed and fail across many organizations and had great insight to offer about the role of leadership in design thinking.

processes, and people. It made no sense to talk about the user's experience without talking about stakeholders *inside* the ATO.

So if designers had to take internal stakeholders into account, were they less important, or more so, than end users? Of course, this should be a false tradeoff, but in many cases it was all too real. My colleague at TU Delft, Frido Smulders, and I analysed the design process in a large automobile manufacturer to explore how designers took internal constituents into account.[4] We found that while the design team members used collaborative workshops and tools such as user personas to understand the needs of the end-users (i.e., drivers), they were less concerned about what internal stakeholders thought. On the contrary, team members treated them with a degree of disdain, describing them as "flatlanders" who could not see beyond their limited view of the world.[5]

Not all design teams bypass internal "users" in this way. But where there are many external and internal "users," which ones you prioritize becomes a real issue.

For Chris Ferguson, reconciling the design teams' user-centred creative-thinking strengths with the needs of the organization was an issue of integration, and this in turn depended on a third issue – leadership: "I think it comes down to 'Who are the leaders?' ... Can they have credibility on the creative front, but also credibility on the business front? It's rare people who can pull off both. And I think if you have one and not the other, you're really going to struggle in that kind of role."

True enough. But as we saw in chapter 3, it was not just about who the leader is: it's also about stability. At Procter and Gamble (P&G), design thinking had a passionate advocate in A.G. Lafley, who retired in 2009; his successor exited the scene after a turbulent four years. Lafley returned in 2013, gave design thinking a boost, and handed over to David Taylor in 2015. Through this period, the leadership of Design at P&G also changed several times.

Under P&G's distributed model, in which design thinking was spread across the business units, leadership of the business units themselves was also critical – and this too was constantly changing. "If you get a new general manager, you get a new president, in general the strategy changes" said Holly O'Driscoll. With these changes, ideas embarked on under the previous leadership could be up for reevaluation.

"User-centred design" is really an oversimplification. The sheer number and variety of stakeholders, all with legitimate interests, means that you can never be completely sure who the real user is and which perspective to take into account. Lack of clarity about who the user is places heavy demands on leadership to integrate the different perspectives. Yet that leadership is often too unstable to be counted on over the long term.

This shifting, ambiguous landscape of stakeholders, leaders, and interested parties gives rise to the Tension of Perspective.

The Impact of the Tension of Perspective

As a result of the Tension of Perspective, great ideas from design thinking programs can flounder at the implementation stage. If projects are implemented, they often end up quite different from the original idea, and far from the user experience envisaged by the design thinking team.

We saw how frequent changes in leadership resulted in organizational inertia at P&G: as business units tacked towards caution, design-led innovations faltered. Other design teams also felt out of step with the rest of their organization. At Pfizer, areas of innovation were shut down because "we were taking these new innovative ideas and spaces and putting them into an organization that was essentially allergic to innovation," said Wendy Mayer. Similarly, at Manulife, Rocky Jain reflected that "the pace at which we're able to solve problems and create solutions has outpaced some of the capacity within Manulife … you create something amazing, but now how do you get this box that you've created onto a moving train?"

In other situations, innovations underwent extensive modifications as they progressed through the implementation system. We saw in chapter 4 how ideas that started out as disruptive innovations could end up incremental, becoming more complex – but less user-centred – as different user groups had their input.

I heard story after story about how innovations were abandoned – or radically changed – once they were exposed to the rest of the organization. Once a design team lost control of an idea, anything could happen to it. Said Brandon Riddell at Canadian Tire, "It wasn't enough for us to just build out our prototypes, chuck it over the fence and hope that they know how to manage it after. A lot of things were being torn apart, rebuilt entirely, and changed in many ways, so they deviated significantly from what our vision was for the product or what the initial prototype was once it had been removed from this environment."

This pattern was typical. On one of my visits to IDEO in San Francisco, I sat down with a former student of mine, David Aycan. A mechanical engineer by training, David is the embodiment of that combination of intellectual, tinkerer, and entrepreneur that makes the Bay Area so stimulating. In his contact with many IDEO clients, he saw how important the internal perspective was.

David's project, Creative Difference,[6] is a tool that measures an organization's creativity and indicates areas for improvement. The tool analyzes the degree to which employees look for inspiration outside the organization and the role of collaboration and empowerment in getting innovations implemented.

The results he had seen reflected the tension. "We see, in a lot of traditional companies, that [the design is] kind of tossed over to engineering, and engineering kind of solves all the little issues from then on, without necessarily being connected to the vision or purpose of the thing."

The message was clear. If design thinkers failed to pay attention to the *other* users of their ideas – the people who had to implement them, often at the cost of huge disruption in their own lives – the ideas could drift far from their original goals, lose momentum, or grind to an ignominious halt.

Managing the Tension of Perspective

Design thinkers have many strategies for managing the Tension of Perspective; none of these could be described as a "slam-dunk," but each has its own advantages and challenges. They boiled down to two directions: loosening control, by handing over "unfinished" innovations that allowed internal stakeholders to design the final product; and extending the reach of designers into the implementation process through various means of collaboration.

Canadian Tire's platform for Christmas lights, as we saw in chapter 4, was one way of loosening control by giving departments the flexibility to do their own innovation. Doing it this way meant that the departments "owned" the innovation and would be more likely to make it happen.

Another way is to hand off prototypes to an implementation arm dedicated to bringing prototypes from the design process into reality. Toronto-Dominion Bank set up a separate 150-person unit for developing technology, not far from its lab at Communitech in Waterloo. "And there will be more" said Craig Haney. "What they understand is that the [innovation] labs play a very specific role. The corporation as it stands is not able to necessarily ingest very well, so they have to build these external teams to help drive that next level of productization of these prototypes."

Organizations with distributed models of design thinking – in which design thinkers were seeded through various departments – were less concerned about project implementation. At P&G, the role of design thinking was not so much to come up with solutions as to train design thinkers who would return to their departments and "infect" them with design approaches and methods. While Holly O'Driscoll cared passionately about solutions, implementation was ultimately the department's responsibility; for her, the real agenda was mindset change.

The ATO also took a "hands-off" approach. Instead of offering direct help with a project when requested, John Body would offer to provide the department with one design facilitator, who would set up a design hub. The hub would in turn become part of the ATO's Community of Practice, broadening the design capability while allowing each department to solve its own problems. Solutions that were homegrown within departments had a greater chance of being implemented.

One downside of this distributed approach is that it doesn't do much to cultivate innovations across the boundaries of an organization. The ATO's Community of Practice went some way towards breaking down silos, though, by creating a common language and encouraging discussion of shared challenges. Yet as the complexity of innovations increases, it becomes ever more critical to engage the various stakeholders across the organization who will be affected by them.

The second way to manage the Tension of Perspective is for designers to become engaged in the implementation process. In this vein, Tim Brown and Roger Martin argued that the path towards implementation is a design task in itself. They wrote about the challenge in a *Harvard Business Review* article in 2015:[7] "... with very complex artifacts, the design of their 'intervention' – their introduction and integration into the status quo – is even more critical to success than the design of the artefacts themselves." For this reason, some design thinkers, instead of loosening control, chose to become *more* involved in implementation. Brown and Martin argued that the design team needs to work intimately with stakeholders, going back and forth with prototypes and insights. Yet while undeniably important, engaging stakeholders is actually very tough to do. With complex innovations, there are just so many of them, and the work of engaging stakeholders takes a patience, flexibility … *and* stubbornness in the right measure.

Designers *do* bring something unique to discussions with internal stakeholders. When I visited MindLab, I liked Christian Bason's way of putting it: "organizational acupuncture," to address the critical pressure points within a system. Designers, Bason told me, could make a unique contribution to the discourse throughout the organization by questioning problem frames and ways of understanding; however, this was a far from simple thing to put into practice.

Though MindLab had mostly concerned itself with policy development, it was steadily doing just what Brown and Martin suggested: taking on the implementation process to a much greater extent by getting the policy and implementation people in the room at the same time and facilitating a constructive discussion. Interesting as all this was, it sounded to me a far cry from what we traditionally think of as design.

Bason conceded the point, but told me a story to illustrate how "traditional" design skills could be useful in this kind of interaction. One of his designer colleagues had just shown him a visualization of the data streams generated in the Danish employment system, educational system, and business-support system. The context had to do with the future of advanced manufacturing in Denmark and how Denmark might be supported as a manufacturing nation. "You know, third industrial revolution and all that," he said.

"Now that's quite a sophisticated discussion, about what governance structures are in place, what policy efforts are in place, and what data is generated." But designers brought something unique to the discussion: "The design skill is to visualize it in a way that is meaningful and understandable across the system." Just to be present at the table, designers at MindLab had to master economics and law, but they also brought unique insights from end users, through ethnographic and anthropologic work, in the form of videos, audio, and notes from for the interviews they had conducted with manufacturing businesses. Designers were storytellers and user advocates within a system that could all too easily become focused on itself.

It goes deeper still. Early in my exploration of design thinking, I interviewed Anna Kindler, then vice provost at the University of British Columbia. Kindler had trained in industrial/graphic design in her native Poland and worked through various professorial roles to end up in senior administration. At the time, I was intrigued by a designer working deep in the bureaucracy of a major university. It flew in the face of my (then) image of the designer as a free spirit who sat uncomfortably with constraints and organizational politics. Her comments formed one of those pivotal light-bulb moments for me. As Bason told me his story, Kindler's comments bubbled to the surface again.

"One of the connections that I see between my training as a designer and my work as a university senior administrator relates to what has always attracted me to design," Kindler told me. "It is the call not only to solve problems but actually to *find* problems that may be addressed even before they surface. My take on the essence of design is that as you walk through life, you actively look at how things can be improved. Being a designer is therefore a mindset as much as a professional capacity. And I believe that the same mindset underpins successful academic leadership."

So designers could bring not only skills and data to the table, but also a distinct perspective. How does this conversation come about? Sadly, it often doesn't.

At Bridgeable in Toronto, one program involved establishing a "Patient Hub" at a drug company to act as a fulcrum for design thinking around patient experience. In spite of efforts to engage other stakeholders, silos endured. Chris Ferguson told me, "I think the rub, or the big challenge, for them is that their stakeholders aren't motivated to collaborate with [design thinkers]. They have their own jobs, right? So their R&D people are focused on R&D. People in patient safety and information are focused on patient safety and information. They have no motivation to go and collaborate with a Patient Hub person."

Yes, that was the rub: on the one hand, you could hand off the implementation to other parts of the organization, but that meant you lost control over the outcome. On the other, you could try to get engaged in the implementation process – and, as a design thinker, you had a lot to offer – but there were strong forces working against you. Nobody seemed to have found the definitive answer to the Tension of Perspective.

The Tension of Perspective, Reframed

Pretty much everyone I spoke to recognized the tension, though they might use different words for it. A few didn't worry much about it – like Holly O'Driscoll, they might define success as mind-set change or perhaps as the number of ideas they helped others develop. Most, however, did see the issue as important, and some reframed the Tension of Perspective through programs that brought the entire organization into the design effort. Another – intriguing – way was to take a systems perspective as well as a user perspective: in effect, to treat the rest of the organization as an implementation system and integrate this with a user-centred perspective.

The key to the first approach, engaging the whole organization, seemed to be strong leadership. Bridgeable's Patient Hub project was an example of a consciously designed "grassroots movement" – along the lines of my earlier discussion with IDEO's Mathew Chow, when he advocated designing "movements" as opposed to top-down "mandates."

The Patient Hub was seen as an integrator team, charged with working across the organization to provide a patient perspective. The team included individuals who also belonged to specific functions, such as R&D, marketing, etc. Yet as we've seen, the silos persisted.

Contrast this with Bridgeable's other project, for a different drug company. In this case, "We were brought in by the CEO and the executive team; it was a very top-down process. Essentially, what we did was we worked with the CEO and the management team to hijack the brand planning process," said Chris Ferguson. The team mandated the use of design tools, under Bridgeable's guidance, for brand planning.

Neither approach was perfect. "I think the big pro of the Patient Hub, the organic, kind of grassroots approach, was their ability to work on specific projects and show specific deliverables," he told me. As we saw earlier, though, it was still tough to engage the other departments. "The con is, it's … not uniform across the entire organization. If [other departments] want to do it, they do it; if they don't, they don't."

However, the top-down approach could become a "checkbox" process. "They'll say, 'Okay, I did my journey map. Okay. Well, I prototyped some ideas with some external stakeholders.' It's broad-reaching and it's consistent, but is it as impactful? In a lot of cases, I don't see it being as impactful."

If neither approach was 100 percent successful in engaging the organization, was there a model that integrated top-down and bottom-up approaches? Pfizer's Dare to Try program seemed to have elements of both – we saw in chapter 3 how it had been successful in mobilizing the organization and changing its culture.

The program started out conventionally enough. "There was a senior leader," Wendy Mayer told me, "that was a very strong advocate and sponsor, because he felt like he kept telling his organization to be more innovative, but they weren't coming up with new ideas. He was getting very frustrated."

He designed a program, at the time called Disciplined Experimentation, to empower people to come up with ideas, and Mayer's innovation team worked with him to roll it out across his division. At that small scale, it was effective. "It worked so well … that the CEO [Ian Read] actually saw some of the output, and he said, 'I want to be able to have this capability across the organization.'" It was renamed Dare to Try, and expanded.

Dare to Try had three essential elements: creative problem solving, design thinking, and Lean Experimentation. The latter involved developing prototype ideas, assessing where there might be potential, identifying the underlying assumptions and success factors, doing quick experiments, being prepared to pivot if the hypotheses are not supported, and further iteration and development of ideas.

The program seemed to combine the design and implementation perspectives. But scaling up an initiative like this was not easy: people don't feel empowered just because the CEO says so.

Then serendipity intervened. In 2014, Pfizer attempted a combination with AstraZeneca. Although the attempt wasn't successful, it brought out the best in Read. Mayer told me what happened next.

"The CEO actually sent out a note company-wide … to say that AstraZeneca was his Dare to Try. That was huge, because it really helped people see that this is something that, even all the way up to the CEO, people are thinking about, and he wasn't successful, and that it was okay, but it was still important that he tried; and that he tried to bring in new thinking of how to approach some of the challenges that we face as an organization."

Not many CEOs can – or would dare – to turn a situation like this into an invitation to the rest of the organization to fail too and learn from it. The Dare to Try program energized Pfizer and got people across the organization speaking the language of innovation.

Facing up to a major challenge managed to turn design thinking into both a directive and a grassroots movement at the same time. What seemed important was that the senior leadership had not just *mandated* design thinking, but *adopted* it, role modelled it, and invited others to adopt it too.

This was an inspiring story of engaging the whole organization; but all the while, I was conscious of the rocky journeys the ATO and P&G had experienced. In both cases, interest was highly dependent on the sustained commitment of senior leadership. In both cases, design thinking had floundered when leadership changed. Was there another way of bridging the divide between design thinking and implementation? One that didn't depend on who was in charge?

In effect, I was looking for a different model of design thinking, one that engaged *both* the user and the organization at the same time. That's when I met Alex Ryan.

It would take another book to discuss Ryan's ideas, and as it happens he is writing one.[8] I'll do my best to capture our conversation here.

Ryan describes himself as a "public servant by day, entrepreneur by night." Before moving to Toronto in 2017 to take over the leadership of the MaRS Solutions Lab, he co-founded and directed Alberta CoLab,* a seven-person team with the Department of Energy in Alberta, Canada. He also founded and runs a boutique consultancy, Synthetikos. Alberta CoLab uses design thinking, but its approach is not the same as the human-centred design promoted by IDEO and other design firms.

---

*   Not to be confused with IDEO's CoLab, mentioned in previous chapters.

Ryan's winding journey into design thinking began in defence research with the Defence Science and Technology Organisation in Australia. While there, he completed a PhD at the University of Adelaide in complex systems and applied mathematics, and helped develop a concept of adaptive campaigning, which applied insights from adaptive systems theory to complex warfare.

Invited to visit the U.S. Army's elite School of Advanced Military Studies (SAMS), he sat in on a systemic operations design practicum. It had a profound effect on him. "I was fascinated," he wrote later.[9] "Over the past decade, I had observed and participated in dozens of army planning exercises, and read about hundreds more. This was almost exactly like none of them." Students, with the encouragement of instructors, were discussing meaning and alternative logical frames, visualizing problems, thinking critically, debating, engaging around their deepest disagreements.

At the centre of the process was the larger-than-life Shimon Naveh. A brigadier general (reserve) in the Israeli military, Naveh is a legendary figure in military intellectualism. His theory of systemic operational design applies system theory to military problems. System theory analyzes the elements of a system, such as a community or an operational unit, looking at the relations between these elements and the operation of the system as a whole. Naveh's work draws on diverse fields such as postmodern philosophy, literary theory, architecture, and psychology. Not known for either the simplicity of his ideas or his modesty, he commented in an interview in 2007, "[My doctrine] is not easy to understand; my writing is not intended for ordinary mortals."[10]

Captivated, Ryan returned to Australia and read everything he could find related to the workshop and Naveh's ideas. It was an eclectic list that included military operations, philosophy, complexity theory, systems thinking ... and design thinking. He joined the SAMS faculty in 2008, the first non-U.S. civilian ever to serve on it.

In Ryan's three years at SAMS, the team graduated 600 colonels and majors educated in design. As a SAMS faculty member and later a consultant with Booz Allen Hamilton, Ryan explored design further.

All this led to a fresh perspective on design thinking. In our interview, Ryan talked of "systemic design" as a way to integrate systems thinking and design thinking. This idea of bringing the two fields together was grounded in theories like soft systems methodology and critical systems thinking.[11] It was certainly a different approach from design thinking as practised in organizations.

Ryan was critical of the way design thinking is applied to complex, systemic problems.* "Design thinking" he told me, "has moved upstream into more systemic challenges, but a lot of the product assumptions are still embedded in the basic techniques that a design thinking approach brings."

He was talking about user-centred design and making the point that, for some problems, the idea of a single "user" is inappropriate. Since his work is in the public sector, this was his frame of reference. "Often people talk about user-centered design," he said, "but a government policy doesn't really have users. [It] has many different stakeholders and right holders." What mattered was not just the end-user, but the entire network of stakeholders and the relationships between them: the *system*, in other words.

He went on. "Designers tend to want to leap into action and work on something that's really cool, that's really desirable to an end user, but in doing so they can often act on a point in the system that's not really strategic; it's not going to be a leverage point. So stepping back and mapping the system helps you to identify better the leverage points where design could really make a difference."

---

* Essentially, wicked problems, as we discussed in chapter 2.

Ryan was not denying the value of design thinking but arguing that it was incomplete without systems thinking. As a public-sector innovator, he was talking about stakeholders in a broad sense – citizens, interest groups, and communities – but I could see that his arguments also applied to stakeholders within any large organization.

In a 2014 paper,[12] Ryan and co-author Mark Leung of the Rotman School of Management (whom we first met in chapter 3) compared two projects, one at the University of Toronto and the other in the Government of Alberta; the former applying design thinking, and the latter using a systems approach based on the U.S. Army's methodology. Ryan and Leung found that the two disciplines had a great deal to learn from each other: "We believe the similarities of the two methodologies provide a common ground on which to build a more centered [*sic*] approach to systemic design, while the differences provide opportunities for learning and improving both methodologies."[13] What did the difference look like? The University of Toronto project, undertaken by Rotman DesignWorks, sought to improve adherence by faculty and staff to the university's procurement process. As a starting point, the design team identified faculty and staff as the "users" of the system and sought to provide value by meeting their needs. The team shadowed more than twenty faculty and staff and developed personas – depictions of archetypal users – to empathize with their perspective, as shown in Figure 5.3.

Through design methods such as this, the Rotman design team focused on the stories they heard from users and reframed the problem as one of repositioning procurement as a trusted advisor rather than an enforcer of policy. This was followed by a series of co-creation workshops, in which the design team and users developed experience maps and prototypes of possible solutions. These prototypes were discussed with a broader group of users and modified,

Dr. Wong
'Academic Maverick'

"One experiment and the world changes."

Christine
'In the Trenches'

"We are people too...not just databases."

User Needs

emotional
FREEDOM AND FLEXIBILITY TO EXPRESS MY INDIVIDUALITY

social
BUILD COLLABORATIVE RELATIONSHIPS

practical
DEMONSTRATE VALUE FOR MONEY

PROVIDE A SAFETY NET TO PROTECT ME FROM RISKS

communication
KEEP INFORMATION SIMPLE AND ACCESSIBLE

5.3 Personas used in the Rotman DesignWorks project on University of Toronto procurement

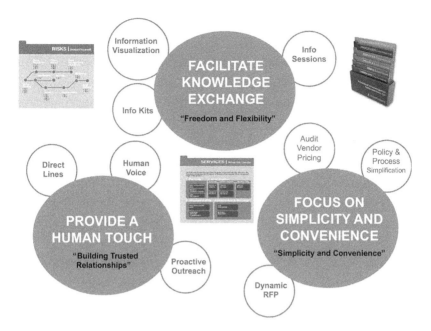

5.4 The activity system proposed by the Rotman DesignWorks team

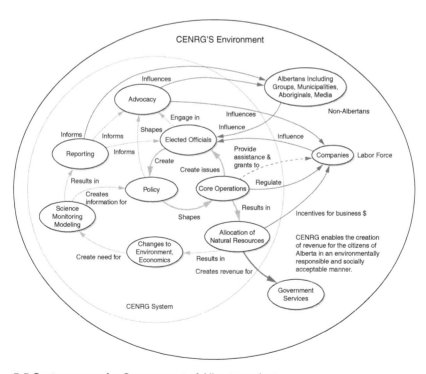

5.5 Systems map for Government of Alberta project

in an iterative process, to arrive at a solution. It was a classic, user-centred, design thinking approach.

The team's ultimate recommendation was a comprehensive "activity system" (Figure 5.4) encompassing a human touch, knowledge, and simplicity and convenience.

The project for the Government of Alberta Clean Energy and Natural Resources Group (CENRG), on the other hand, took a systems perspective. This project was about improving the effectiveness and efficiency of the approach to managing natural resources. Here, a group of civil servants was led through a process that involved understanding the relationships between different stakeholders, using tools such as stakeholder maps and affinity diagramming. A systems map developed for this project is shown in Figure 5.5.

The end result was a vision of transformed values and their implications, shown in Figure 5.6, along with systems that would support the change, oppose it, and provide resources.

The proposed solution represented a voluntary shift from an individualistic mentality to a more collaborative one. The group also developed an operational approach to translate the plan into action, mapping out the resources that might be brought to bear to support or oppose the change, along with a system of those actors who might work to support the change and those who might oppose it.

The two projects showed how design thinking and systems thinking were different but could be complementary. Rotman's design thinking approach put user needs before solutions and focused on empathy with users, physical prototyping, rapid testing, and user feedback. The Alberta CoLab approach, by contrast, emphasized systems mapping, exploring mental models, theoretical grounding, and narrating the journey of learning while integrating education with practice.

I was intrigued. Here was a possible resolution of my discomfort around Buchanan's dictum at the ATO. By integrating design

5.6 Vision developed with the CENRG

VALUES IN USE	ACTION STRATEGIES	PATTERNS	CONSEQUENCES
Risk tolerant	Question guidance	Important over urgent	Stronger collective vision
Embrace complexity	Slow down to speed up	Risk-tolerant leadership	Meaningful change
Government of Alberta identity	Purposeful action, strategic influence	Growing understanding	Communities of practice
Transparency	Continuous learning	Continual adaptation	Development pathways
Security and stability	Fight for the collective	Growing trust	
Control information by exception	Shared accountability / shared reward		
Succession planning	Collaboration as reward		

thinking and systems thinking, organizations could be *both* user-centred and system-centred at the same time. The implementation system within large organizations was one such system, and understanding its constraints, leverage points, and potential synergies needed to be as much a part of design as understanding the end user. Just as external stakeholders and their interrelationships could be consulted and mapped, internal "users" of an innovation could be planned for and built into design work.

While systems thinking could bring a broader perspective to design, design could bring storytelling to systems thinking. Designers often develop "user personas," vivid stories about users; if they took full account of internal stakeholders, they could develop similar stories for them:* no more Flatland, but instead thoughtful attention to those who influenced, and were influenced by, the outcome.

Dr Ofri's dilemma came to mind. True, she could not help her patient without understanding his world. But equally, she could not help him without taking into account the system that could aid or hinder him: relationships between specialists, therapists, educational programs, equipment, drug providers, and many others. Patient empathy alone was not enough. But combined with a deep and broad appreciation of systems, it might reduce the pain of the Tension of Perspective.

---

* In our paper, Frido Smulders and I called these "disciplinas."

PART 3   **REFRAMING DESIGN THINKING FOR YOUR ORGANIZATION**

reframing design thinking

Luxury Liners and Small Craft

Railtown is a trendy neighbourhood in the otherwise depressed Downtown Eastside of Vancouver, BC, Canada. Nestled cheek-by-jowl alongside low-rent apartment buildings, safe injection sites, and hostels for the homeless, its fashionably renovated warehouses have attracted a quirky mix of artists, software entrepreneurs, wine bars ... and designers.

Every one of these design studios is small, some tiny. One of the larger studios is Dossier Creative, which specializes in packaging, branding, and innovation. Located in a former canning plant, Dossier's studio is an open area of about 5,000 square feet facing the industrial port and, beyond it, a sweeping view of the coastal mountains.

A total of fifteen employees occupy the space. There is one meeting room and a brainstorming room; otherwise, the studio is open plan. One of the co-founders, Ronna Chisolm, occupies the only office; her husband and the other co-founder, Don Chisolm, works at an open desk with the rest of the team. Tables are littered with scalpels, Sharpies, semi-finished sketches, and mocked-up packages (Figure 6.1).

6.1 Dossier's studio in Vancouver, Canada. Images provided by Dossier.

That's it. That's the entire company. It couldn't be a further cry from the world of large corporations and government. Ronna Chisolm captured the vibe at Dossier:

> As a small organization, we can be agile, change and pivot fast. When we wanted to create a business and design intern lab (Railyard*), we just did it – knowing we can test, iterate, and evolve it. When we wanted to move into partnering with companies in design ventures and launching our own venture – we could just make it happen. We've had to be lean and entrepreneurial to evolve over thirty years.

Design thinking grew up in places like this. Compared with large organizations, small studios like Dossier are like crossing the ocean

---

*   Dossier's internship program in social innovation. http://railyardlab.com/.

in a small fishing boat as opposed to a luxury liner. Life can be turbulent, fast moving, and unpredictable, and the only way to survive is to be nimble.

Large organizations can be interesting and stimulating places to work; nimble they are not. Frustration with this aspect of corporate life – and with the challenge from smaller competitors – has led many CEOs to seek new, more fluid ways of working, such as "intrapreneurship," and to adopt senseless maxims like "ready, fire, aim." And to embrace design thinking.

The frustration is understandable, and indeed I believe that design thinking has much to offer large organizations. But the challenge of implementing it should not be underestimated.

It doesn't help that nobody can agree on what design thinking is. This is a field that has been built through practice; theory is scrambling to catch up. Is it reasonable, for example, to suggest that designers of oil rigs think the same way as fashion designers? That all designers subscribe to a human-centred view of the world? (They don't.) Just what is the common thread that defines design thinking? Like design itself, design thinking eludes definition.

As we saw in chapter 2, misconceptions abound. Though design thinking is often seen as a recent fad, the term has been used by designers for decades.[1] It is seen as being all about creative thinking, but it is less about crazy ideas than reflective practice.[2] It is not just a toolkit you can readily adopt, but a distinct way of seeing and being in the world.[3] Nor is it a quick fix: successful organizational design thinking initiatives take years to mature. Misconceptions like these make it more difficult for organizational design thinkers to set and adhere to a reasonable set of expectations. In this chapter, I don't hope to provide a precise definition of design thinking:

such a definition would inevitably fall short of capturing the myriad ways it is applied in practice.

Can you turn a luxury liner into a small fishing boat? Certainly not; nor would you want to. Fortunately, however, the challenges of applying design thinking are predictable; I will suggest three ways of *thinking* about design thinking – of reframing it – to address the three tensions, as some organizations described in this book have done. In the process, I will offer some suggestions for your organization to take advantage of the experience of those who have sailed these waters. To help you navigate, you'll find a summary of my recommendations in Figure 6.2.

Reframe 1: Design Thinking as a Mindset – Escape, Model, Prototype

In chapter 3, we saw how the Tension of Inclusion can be reframed as a question of *mindset.*

Designers are all about balancing possibility with practicality. Unlike the act of pure creation that we associate with fine art, the essence of design is making useful things.* The process of getting there requires an open mind, a sense of optimism, and a willingness to suspend reality, temporarily.

What does this look like in organizations? Design thinking can provide an escape from the systemic, political, and cultural constraints that stifle thought in many organizations. It can be modelled as a cultural movement. And it can be prototyped and scaled up.

---

*   Not confined to material things: services and processes are also designed.

6.2 Reframing Design Thinking: Summary

Reframe 1: Design Thinking as a Mindset	Escape from the Dominant Mindset	1. *Create a distinct space and location* for design thinking: a safe space where ideas can flow freely.
		2. *Develop reflective practice*, where people don't just practise design thinking but reflect on it together.
		3. Have an outreach program to engage the organization in creative ways.
	Model Your Mindset	1. Leaders need a strong understanding of *design thinking* to become strong advocates.
		2. Open the Black Box: Take the "mystery" out of the process for the rest of the organization.
	Prototype the Mindset	1. *Build and protect the mindset:* articulate a "design attitude," not just a process.
		2. *Create movements, not mandates:* Top-down gets you only so far. Develop grassroots support.
Reframe 2: Design Thinking As a Platform	Technological Platforms	1. *Design choices, not solutions:* Build platforms for others to refine according to their own needs.
		2. *Develop and nurture "activators"* – people who can spark design across the organization.
	Collaborative Platforms	1. *Multilateral collaboration:* Work with cross-functional teams.
		2. *Community of practice:* In distributed models, regularly bring together those who are interested in design thinking.
Reframe 3: Design Thinking within a Bigger System	Internal Stakeholders	1. *Treat internal stakeholders as users:* Understand internal departments' needs and contexts as you would those of end users.
		2. *Actively engage them:* Hand the design process over to those who will have to implement the results.
		3. *Fail, reflect, and learn together:* Involve them throughout the process, not just at the start or the end.
	External Stakeholders	1. *Integrate and collaborate:* Invite outsiders – collaborators and even competitors – into your design process.
		2. *Focus on leverage points in the system:* Think beyond the end user to consider the broader internal and external ecosystems.
		3. *Include abstract stakeholders:* Think beyond people to include the planet, communities, and society.

Escape from the Dominant Mindset

There are several ways of using design as an escape valve.

1 **Create a distinct space and location**: Most of the labs I interviewed had a dedicated space that was physically different from the rest of the organization, and provided a relaxed and open vibe. At Procter & Gamble (P&G), there was even a "space-within-a-space": the green carpet, where participants could speak openly without fear of reprisal.

   If the space is an escape from the routine, it should not be too far away. Canadian Tire's lab was a two-hour drive from its head office, which created difficulties in recruiting participants. MindLab's and P&G's spaces were located outside the main office but within easy reach.

A Safe Space

Whether your program is centralized or decentralized, you should have a dedicated space, as did almost every organization I spoke to. A physical space signals to the organization that it is committed to design thinking, provides a place where workshop participants can freely speak their mind, and gives them the opportunity to focus on the problem with minimal interruption.

Some of the spaces I visited were designed to appear different from traditional office spaces – MindLab's submarine-like "Mind" and P&G's former brewery at clay street are good examples – and this was no accident. As soon as they walked in, participants understood that their meeting would not be business as usual.

Most of all, your design thinking space should make participants feel safe: keep it physically separate from the main
office – but not too far away, so that you're not disconnected from
the organization.

Your space should be designed to encourage the flow of ideas,
and this means making it *egalitarian*: get rid of corner offices and
rectangular meeting tables. It should be *flexible* to allow for an iterative, sometimes unpredictable process: have mobile furniture that
you can move around at will. Participants should feel free to make
their ideas tangible and physical: make sure rough *prototyping*
materials are within easy reach. Finally, have *"focus"* spaces within
the space so that teams can work closely together on a problem.

---

2 **Develop reflective practice**: The Australian Tax Office (ATO)
created a Community of Practice: a forum where design thinkers
across the organization could meet regularly to share their challenges and experiences. In other organizations with a distributed
design thinking model, opportunities for sharing experiences
were no less important, but were less formal. Many design
studios I know, including Dossier, take time out to discuss their
practice and bring in new learning.

If design is reflective practice, it makes sense to reflect regularly on how it is working. When things are busy, it is difficult
to carve out time for reflection; at the ATO, these sessions were
held early in the morning.

3 **Have an outreach program**: Many design thinking initiatives,
even highly centralized ones, make conscious efforts to reach out
to other parts of the organization and to external communities.

The Mayo Clinic's annual *Transform* conference is a major event that brings health care innovators together. MindLab's staff publish research and travel internationally to present at conferences.

I had expected that private-sector organizations would be extremely protective of their knowledge about innovation and design thinking; I was surprised to find many to be extremely open. While many such organizations have well-developed internal programs, there is an opportunity to go further still and sponsor design thinking conferences and other such outreach programs. This can open up the company to discovering new knowledge, exchanging best practices, and developing interesting networks.

Should You Centralize or Decentralize Design Thinking in Your Organization?

Whether you have a central lab or distribute design thinking throughout the organization depends on your goals. If you are primarily trying to develop a design mindset, a distributed model has its advantages; if you are mostly concerned with disruptive innovation, you will prefer a central lab that is connected externally. However, in the organizations I spoke to, almost all – even those with distributed programs like P&G – had some form of central lab that acted as home base.

Being centralized has some advantages:

You can control and preserve the integrity of the process.
You can develop in-house expertise on the design thinking prooose.

You can sponsor research and continuous learning about design thinking and methods.

You can provide an escape valve for operating departments.

You can do exploratory, cross-functional or "platform" work that doesn't reside in departments.

However, there are advantages to a distributed program:

Your design work is closer to the action, more grounded in reality and should be easier to implement as a result.

Operating units own the projects and are therefore more committed to them.

You can build a common language across departments to discuss how work gets done.

You can work to foster a design mindset throughout the organization.

Cindy Tripp at P&G was a strong advocate of a distributed approach: "When you have a central group ... you would never get past the quick win, because businesses are always going for the quick win," she said.

Still, a good deal depends on the amount of autonomy and responsibility your operating units have. At P&G, business units were expected to develop disruptive innovations within their own areas, so having a distributed approach worked well with the goal of disruptive innovation. For situations in which operating units are not responsible for innovation, as in many public-sector organizations, you may need a centralized approach to bring about disruption. I'll have more to say on this topic in the final chapter.

Model Your Mindset

Many organizations see design thinking as a vehicle for shifting their culture in the direction of customer centricity and creativity. Culture change is never an easy task, and the while a "design mindset" is a worthy goal, it needs to be made actionable for those who are not familiar with the idea. People need to see what the mindset actually is and what it means to them. Here are two basic considerations if your organization is framing the challenge in this way.

1 **Leaders need a strong understanding of design thinking**: The survival of design thinking depends critically on support of leaders, and a surface understanding leaves it vulnerable to hostile forces within the organization. Design thinking has been criticized as a "fad" by some in the business community, perhaps in reaction to the level of hype it has received; what can be underappreciated is the level of depth and rigour that design thinkers bring to innovation.

   To develop this understanding, A.G. Lafley brought the P&G executive team to San Francisco for a workshop at IDEO. This investment of time was an important foundation for the company's design thinking initiative. The Mayo Clinic Center for Innovation (CFI) brought together a team of high-profile design thinkers and consultants to act as advisors.

2 **Open the Black Box**: For those new to it, design thinking can be shrouded in mystery. Perhaps that is part of the attraction, different as it is from the normal way of doing things. Yet the image of design thinkers as "those crazy cowboys" (as at Canadian Tire) is not unusual and underscores the risk of isolation from the organization.

Most design initiatives publish a process diagram that encapsulates the key steps in their process while emphasizing its iterative nature.[4] However, the organizations I spoke to described a process that, while systematic, is far from standardized. In the past, MindLab had published its approach, but by the time I spoke with Christian Bason, it had ceased to do so because it led to oversimplification of design as a linear process.

Regardless of whether you choose to publish a specific process, there is a need to demystify design thinking for the organization. You should make its underlying logic transparent and demonstrate how it integrates creativity, empathy, and reflection. The Advent calendar MindLab developed for one of its ministries was an appealing way of demonstrating the "agile" concept. Similarly inventive ways can be found to bring design thinking into everyday conversation.

Prototype the Mindset

The idea of prototyping – trying things out on a small scale and learning from them – is just as relevant to design thinking programs in organizations as it is to the design process itself. In creating your prototype, here are two central things you should build in.

1 **Build and protect the mindset**: Design thinking is less a set of methods than a way of seeing and being in the world: this idea of a design "mindset" came up again and again in my research. According to IDEO, design thinkers are not just creative, but also optimistic, empathetic, willing to learn from failure, comfortable with ambiguity, and confident.[5] I also found that design thinkers

are highly rigorous – though, as we saw at the Mayo Clinic, they interpret rigour in a very different way from scientists.

To build and communicate a design mindset, you need to be very clear on what it is and what it could mean in your organization. Though the field is relatively new, there are several excellent design researchers who have been grappling for some time with the problem of defining design as a way of thinking. As a starting point, I recommend reading and reflecting on the work of design researchers such as Richard Buchanan, Nigel Cross, and Kees Dorst. For a management perspective, I recommend Sara Beckman, Jeanne Liedtka, and Roger Martin.

2 **Create movements, not mandates**: All the design thinking initiatives I encountered had top management support. Some, like MindLab, had actually been instigated by senior managers who had a passion for design thinking. This support, while necessary, was not sufficient for success. The ATO, P&G, and others had experienced ups and downs in interest in design thinking as organizational leadership changed.

Mathew Chow at IDEO spoke to me of social movements as a model for spreading design thinking in organizations. Chris Ferguson's experience with building grassroots initiatives supported this idea of a bottom-up approach. The task of senior management is to create room for design thinking – in the form of budgets and moral support – but from the beginning, you need to engage constituencies from the ground up.

Developing stories of success helps. I consistently heard about successful labs that initially went after "low-hanging fruit" – quick wins that got people talking, and from there developed a series of case histories they could use to engage the organization. Quick wins like these are readily available in most organizations; a simple reframe can dramatically transform a project and demonstrate the power of design thinking. The TELUS team started with a low-risk employee-engagement project, using the project as a way of getting fellow employees involved with design thinking to help them understand and talk about it; the success of this and other early projects helped get the TELUS Service Design team off the ground and set it on its way.

Reframe 2: Design Thinking as a Technological or Collaborative Platform

"Design platforms, not products" is a familiar design maxim. We saw in chapter 4 how design thinkers were reframing the Tension of Disruption by creating two types of platforms: technological and collaborative.

In *Ten Types of Innovation,*[6] Larry Keeley and his colleagues comment that technology companies build platforms for innovation by others; a good example of this would be Apple's App Store. This strategy is well-established with the tech sector and is emerging in other sectors: the online crowdfunding platform Kickstarter, for example, provides a platform for creative projects. This approach can be used within organizations too: design thinking units can act as internal platform builders and allow individual divisions to elaborate on their ideas.

By taking incremental innovations as an opportunity to build *technological* platforms, design thinkers are providing concrete results while allowing individual departments to take the lead within their own spheres. Meanwhile, they are responding to the imperative to bring about more fundamental change.

Collaborative platforms, however, collect a diverse array of stakeholders who bring knowledge from different perspectives. Part of the design thinker's job is to find these different perspectives – from suppliers, users, even competitors – bring them together and integrate them into a coherent innovation.

Of course they're not independent from each other. Technological platforms provide a vehicle for collaboration, and collaborative platforms can lead to technology platforms. The following are some guidelines for developing and maintaining these platforms.

Technological Platforms

Technological platforms are big ideas that facilitate small ideas. In essence, you are doing the initial work and allowing your divisions to build innovations of their own in the areas they know best. If you are building technological platforms, you should consider the following:

1 **Design choices, not solutions**: There's value in *not* completely solving problems. By allowing internal clients to come up with their own answers, you help create ownership of the ideas – which has the added bonus of helping defuse the Tension of Perspective and increasing the chance of implementation. There are other advantages to stopping short of a full solution: rather than try to take a deep dive into every problem, your design thinking program can focus on developing technology that will be helpful across a range of innovation problems.

   Technology platforms are not restricted to tech companies or retailers of tech products like Canadian Tire. Unilever, for example, used its patent for "fragrance and encapsulated odour counteractant,"[7] to develop global deodorant brands like Axe, Impulse, Rexona, and Sure. Each of these brands uses the same underlying technology to serve different markets in different parts of the world.

2 **Develop and nurture "activators"**: In stopping short of full solutions you still need to have a deep, intimate understanding of the end user, the technological and competitive landscape, and have a vision for the ultimate application of your platform. This means that your design thinking unit needs both to collaborate closely with departments that may use the platform and contribute ideas they may not have considered.

The term "activator" is used at Communitech and refers to the role of the lab director as a catalyst for change within the organization. A good lab director needs to be a *problem finder* who can identify opportunities for technologies that solve multiple problems across the organization. This means being not just a competent designer or a leader of a creative team: the activator must understand the global context, the possibilities inherent in the technology, engage the rest of the organization, and connect people.

Activators and Multipliers: Connect and Scale

An activator is a design thinker who acts as a spark to ignite innovation across the company. He or she may be the director of an internal innovation lab, though in the organizations I interviewed, the term could be applied to any of the team who worked with internal departments.

Says Craig Haney of Communitech, the activator is "as much a business development professional as they are a technology professional, because they are trying to seek problems within the organization" that have the potential for developing platforms.

By connecting across the organization, activators could look for platforms that solved multiple problems: multipliers, in Haney's terms. "Every large organization is siloed to some level. If you can get the activator working within multiple groups within the organization, they can create these multipliers where one solution solves many problems within the organization."

The people I interviewed had their own individual strengths, but the ability to work collaboratively with their client departments and to bring a broad, integrative perspective was common to all of them. Activators need to be clear on the organization's innovation goals, deeply understand its technology, and stay in touch with social and technological trends. You should bring activators within your organization together regularly to share their experiences and stories; it is also a good idea to connect activators across different organizations to expose them to new perspectives.

Collaborative Platforms

Multiple perspectives bring more ideas to the table. Design thinking thrives on collaboration, and the positive, open-minded nature of the design thinkers I interviewed helped invite contributions from all sides. A design thinking program can create links across functional areas within business units and across different business units; it can act as a platform for collaboration by bringing people together in a shared space, and by creating communities of practice.

1 **Multilateral collaboration**: A design thinking workshop gives an organizational unit the opportunity to bring different

perspectives to bear on a common problem. I saw this at work at P&G, where a session to develop ideas for the fabric-softener category included representatives from sales, R&D, and marketing. Each could comment on the feasibility of different approaches and contribute ideas of their own.

You can also have collaboration across organizational units that may be dealing with different problems. In this case, the discussion can encompass technological platforms, as discussed earlier, and also the practice of innovation itself – best practices in ethnographic research, brainstorming; experience with specific design methods, etc.

Organizations often bring users into the design process through a process of collaborative (or participatory) design. This has pros and cons. It can help the team innovate in real time, trying out prototypes and getting instant responses; for some innovations, user-designers can act as ambassadors for new products. On the other hand, users often have trouble envisaging possibilities for innovation early in the process. For this reason, organizations typically involve users selectively, at stages when their input is particularly useful.

2 **Community of practice**: As design thinking catches on, design facilitators can get very busy. It's important from time to time to step away from solving specific problems and talk about the innovation process itself, the challenges they're facing, and what they're learning.

This is particularly important in distributed models, where design thinkers are spread throughout the organization. For the ATO, which did not establish an identifiable lab, regular Community of Practice sessions were particularly important in building a sense of cohesion and shared learning among design thinkers. Yet even in more "centralized" design labs, such as those at the Mayo Clinic and MindLab, design facilitators spend a great deal of time working with operating departments. The learning they gain about design mindset, process, and methods is hugely valuable to other facilitators and is shared regularly.

Reframe 3: Design Thinking Within a Bigger System

We saw in chapter 5 how the Tension of Perspective could be addressed by integrating a "systems" view with user-centred design. In effect, this means understanding problems both broadly *and* narrowly, incorporating the interests of those with a stake in the system as well as the direct users of the design. There are two important groups: *internal* stakeholders within your organization and *external* system players, including end users.

Many of the design thinkers I spoke to were not designers by profession, but executives from other parts of the organization who had developed a passion for this way of approaching problems. Yet it is all too easy for design thinkers – even former executives – to develop a "fortress" mentality, a belief that they alone truly understand users.

Internal stakeholders such as manufacturing, human resources, and sales constitute the organizational ecosystem that surrounds design team. Designers tend to think of them as a *delivery system* to the end user – but they are much more than that. They have deep understanding of the technology, people, and relationships. They also have influence and leverage where it matters. And they have opinions. They are not just a critical element in implementing ideas, but a diverse user group in themselves whose perspectives need to be built into the design process.

There is also an external ecosystem: wholesalers, retailers, and services that make the user experience possible. GE's Adventure

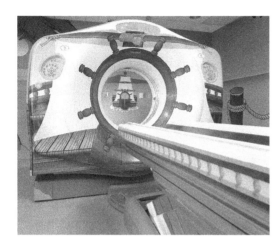

6.3 GE's "Pirate Island" MRI from the Adventure Series
Credit: GE Healthcare

Series[8] is a range of medical-imaging products based on pirate ships and jungle adventures (Figure 6.3). Going through an MRI can be stressful and intimidating for children, often at a confusing, frightening time in their lives. By making a "game" out of the experience, the GE machines can help reduce fear. They cost more than normal MRIs, however, so GE needs to bring hospital administrators on board: one argument for this group is that reduced fear means less sedation and lower costs. GE also needs to engage hospital staff to bring the fantasy alive[9] by role-playing and setting the scene.

The delivery system is not the only external system. Complementary products and services can enhance the experience; competition can detract from it. Social movements, technology, and legislative issues all need to be considered. Because these are critical and changing all the time, you need to understand how key external stakeholders are framing the issues.

Here are some ways of thinking about internal and external stakeholders.

Internal Stakeholders

Internal stakeholders are a "user" group, and though their interests may differ from those of end users, it can be helpful to think of them this way. They need to be engaged in the design process, not treated as an afterthought. Your design thinking team and internal implementation team can use design methods to reflect together on the nature of the problem and its system implications.

1 **Treat internal stakeholders as users**: Internal stakeholders can make or break a project. They can be the carriers of stories that build commitment; they can find and influence leverage points; they can obtain the necessary budget and resources to make the project a reality. Yet they are often left out of the design process.

   User-centred designers do everything possible to empathize with the user experience: shadowing users, observing them, interviewing them, and developing personas and mapping their pathway through the experience. In our study of the design process at an automobile manufacturer, Frido Smulders and I saw how the design team orchestrated workshops with drivers, going into great depth about the experience and brainstorming solutions. Although the internal team was involved at selected points, these interactions were more about gaining their buy-in to the design team's agenda than true consultation.

   To treat internal stakeholders as users, you might consider applying some of these same methods of empathizing with them. Spend time walking in their shoes; understand their motivations and the world they live in; develop personas and map their experience, analyse it, and understand the pain points. By gaining an appreciation of the issues involved in implementing the project, you increase the chances of success.

2 **Actively engage them**: Active engagement means more than involving internal users in brainstorming sessions. It means handing the process over to them. I saw this take shape in many different places: MindLab's maxim of "facilitate, don't consult" positioned it as an enabler of innovation, but the process was owned by the department responsible for implementing the project. The Mayo Clinic CFI sent design facilitators to departments for several weeks at a time to work with an internal team. The ATO and P&G spread design thinking through the organization by training design facilitators who return to their own departments.

This approach is not without risk: at P&G, the quality of facilitators was uneven, and spreading design thinking in this way was a slow process that required consistent, unwavering support from the top. Even the best-trained facilitators have to swim upstream in departmental cultures that are hostile to design thinking. So you need to provide ongoing support for internal facilitators too.

3 **Fail, reflect and learn together**: You need to involve internal stakeholders *throughout* the process, not just in parts of it. Reflective practice involves trying something out, watching what happens, learning from the experience, and putting into practice what you have learned.[10] You learn more by failing than by succeeding: that's why design thinkers put so much emphasis on rapid prototyping. You also learn more by seeking different perspectives on what you experience.

Internal stakeholders can both contribute to this learning process and benefit from it. They will usually know where to look for information about factors such as manufacturing processes, logistics, and resources to shed light on what the next prototype might look like. They may also be in touch with the power levers and personalities that are critical to making the project work and will bring this perspective to the team. However, they will benefit by being exposed to real users and using design methods to make sense of what they see.

Deep involvement of internal stakeholders is one of the advantages of a decentralized model, but as we've seen, this model has disadvantages too. If you choose a centralized lab, make sure you have key internal stakeholders engaged throughout your projects.

External Stakeholders

It is important to avoid false trade-offs and find solutions that integrate the different interests of different stakeholders. However, it's a massive task to take account of external systems; the important thing is to understand the critical relationships and links within the various components, and there are tools available for this purpose. You also need to take account of "abstract" stakeholders, such as the environment or society, that do not have a direct voice.

1 **Integrate and collaborate**: To integrate is to combine separate things to make a complete and congruent whole. Some call this synthesis, and it's intimately connected to creativity.[11] Integrative thinking, says Roger Martin, is the ability to resolve the tension between two opposing ideas by coming up with an alternative that has elements of each but is superior to both:[12] the whole is greater than the sum of its parts. It's *both-and*, not *either-or*.
    My research showed that the most common way of integrating different perspectives was through collaboration. Pfizer's approach to lung cancer drug trials shows how an integrative approach can meet the needs of both patients and drug compa-

nies at the same time. In lung cancer research, it is difficult to get enough patients to take part in clinical trials. Instead of competing for patients with other drug firms, Pfizer works with the National Institutes of Health – as well as some of Pfizer's major competitors – on a major trial called Lung Cancer Master Protocol, or Lung-MAP. Lung-MAP uses genomic profiling to match patients to different drug trials. The system matches the right patient to the right trial, saving money, time, and possibly lives.

Pfizer, P&G, Communitech, and many others had an open, collaborative approach to innovation. To innovate across boundaries, you need to invite others in, sometimes even your competitors.

2   **Focus on leverage points in the system**: The term "systems thinking" grew out of engineering systems and has been considered technical, rigid, and difficult to apply to human systems. However, there have been a number of movements within the field in recent decades that are very promising for design thinkers. Among these, Peter Checkland's Soft Systems Methodology[13] relates systems thinking to managerial problems. If you want to understand how systems thinking can be applied to design, Checkland's *Systems Thinking, Systems Practice* is well worth a read.

If you focus only on the individual user, as many human-centred designers tend to do, your solutions may not have the intended impact. You need to situate the product or service in relation to other products and services, sales channels, information channels, payment systems, and so on. You can design an improved admissions process in a hospital, but unless it takes account of the other things staff are doing, of the hospital's information system, of the hospital's physical infrastructure, it will probably not get very far. You need to identify what points in the system are critical for the design to succeed – the critical leverage points – and how they are related to each other.

The technique of Giga-mapping[14] can help you get a macro view of the relationships in a system. A Giga-map is just what the name suggests: an "everything" map that attempts to capture the important forces in a system and the links between them. Figure 6.4 shows a sample, for urban-habitat design. It's massive and complex – because that's what systems often are. I'd suggest going to the website http://systemsorienteddesign. net/index.php/giga-mapping/giga-mapping-samples, where you can find more examples like this and zoom in to see the details.

A map of the organizational ecosystem can help you find leverage points for building a grassroots "movement" around design thinking on the lines of my interview with Mathew Chow at IDEO in chapter 3. In the field of organizational design, the organizational ecosystem is seen as having five components: strategy, structure, processes, rewards, and people.[15] This kind of framework could be a starting point for your thinking about leverage points.*

3 **Include abstract stakeholders**: Systems include people, but not *only* people. There are more abstract stakeholders too. No responsible designer these days ignores the environment or the community. As you broaden the lens, the organizational, social, and environmental context of design thinking come into focus, and effective design means taking *all* of these into account.

---

*   To go deeper on this, you might consider IDEO's extension of this famous model. External-facing factors are purpose, behaviours, offers, and culture, and internal factors include strategy, structure and roles, processes, talent and leadership, incentives, and infrastructure (space and technology).

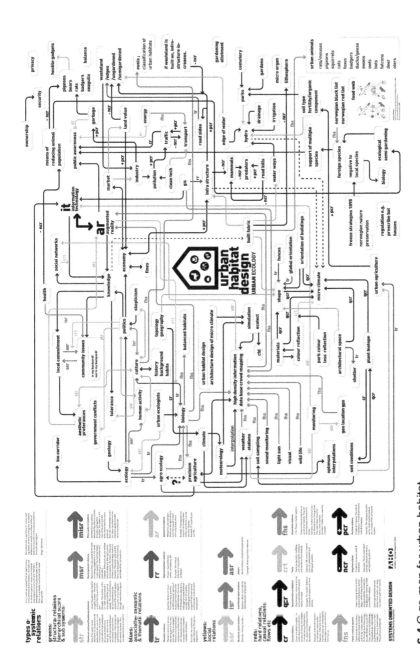

6.4 Gigamap for urban habitat
Credit: Young Eun Choi, Birger Sevaldson, Systems Oriented Design, AHO 2013

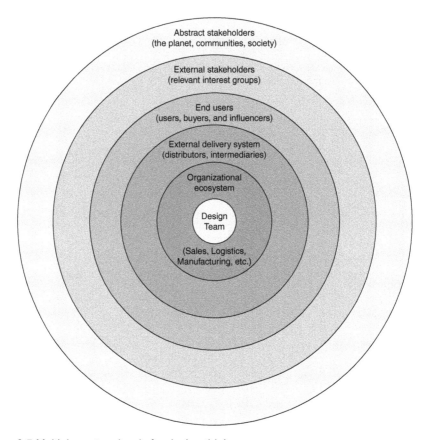

6.5 Multiple system levels for design thinkers

I won't pretend that this is easy. To give you a sense of the complexity here, in Figure 6.5, I've mapped the various stakeholders you need to think about as a set of concentric circles. Fully accounting for all the interests of such a range of stakeholders is a mind-boggling task, and clearly design thinkers need to prioritize. However, you can't prioritize unless you are at least *aware* of the implications of your design across the system as a whole.

It may help you to see this not as imposing new constraints, but creating new opportunities. In 1977, designers Charles and Ray Eames produced a famous video, *Powers of Ten*.[16] It's a fantastic voyage that begins with an everyday scene of a couple having a picnic in a Chicago park. The camera zooms out, each time by a power of 10 metres. We see the couple from further and further away, till the earth itself is invisible in the limitless universe. At 10^{24}, we are 100 million light years away from earth. The camera reverses, zooming in towards the couple and focusing on a spot in the young man's hand, going deeper and deeper in, now into negative powers of 10. At 10^{-16} we are at the level of atoms. The message: everything is linked, and design thinkers themselves are part of a system. There are no limits, only possibilities: the sky is literally the limit.

Above all else, it's this sense of possibility that keeps me intrigued by design thinking. Perhaps large organizations insulate us, as luxury liners do, from possibility in ways that, say, small fishing boats do not. Yet by reframing design thinking, we can make it safer to explore turbulent waters – or, perhaps, we can make ourselves less afraid to get wet.

where do you begin? building your design thinking program

Gerwin Hoogendoorn broke three umbrellas in one week and set out on a quest to make a better umbrella. A.G. Lafley's years in Japan led him to appreciate the power of design; Claudia Kotchka turned him down twice when he asked her to build design into P&G, only to accept his third offer.[1]

There are at least two stories of the origins of the Mayo Clinic Center for Innovation (CFI). In one, Dr Nicholas LaRusso and Dr Michael Brennan, both avid runners, hatched the idea while on a run together. In the other, SPARC emerged over a "twelve-pack of Guinness at Mike Brennan's house."[2]

Storytelling is central to design. Stories bring context to otherwise disconnected facts and help us empathize with users. They provide insight and understanding. They transport us to the decisive moments when choices are made.

Life must be lived forwards, but can only be understood backwards,[3] and stories provide the hindsight needed to interpret experience. Design thinkers are consummate storytellers, and they told me fascinating stories of the challenges they had faced, their wins and their losses. They could look back at their own purpose and role within the organization and their strategies for thriving in what was frequently a hostile environment.

Yet they all had to start by looking forwards: by making critical strategic decisions to get their program going and operational decisions that could have long-term implications. As you consider your own design thinking program, you'll need to think about the questions in this final chapter.

Strategic Decisions

What Is Your Organization's Innovation Strategy and Where Do You Fit?

Your approach to design thinking needs to take account of the broader innovation strategy of your organization. You'll need to take an honest look at what the organization is trying to accomplish, particularly whether your organization is truly ready for disruptive innovation. Experts in the field told me that many executives are attracted by the idea of disruptive innovation but are unwilling or unable to make the drastic organizational changes needed to support it.

Disruptive innovation may be more suited to some industries than others, but there is no clear pattern – in part due to the difficulty in defining what is disruptive. The public-sector programs I encountered tended to be focused on incremental innovation in areas like service delivery and customer experience. Technology and cars seem to be on the verge of technological disruption; this can also be said of more traditional industries like insurance and banking. Even packaged-goods companies like Procter & Gamble (P&G) are interested in disruption, if not in product technology then in business models and strategic alliances.

Many of the programs in this book pursued disruptive innovation by connecting with other stakeholders outside the organization. This can be risky, as it requires a high degree of openness and willingness to share; organizations seem to be driven to it by the alternative risk of standing still in the face of major change. P&G's aggressive, multifaceted innovation strategy emphasizes external connections, as do those of Pfizer, Canadian Tire, and others.

What Are Your Program's Goals?

This may surprise you, but design thinking programs aren't just about innovation. For some, such as the Australian Tax Office (ATO), it's about building a more outside-in culture; for others, such as Canadian Tire, technological innovation looms large. As we saw in chapter 2, innovation is important, but the goals I came across reflected a bigger agenda, encompassing culture and ways of working together:

Facilitate innovation: MindLab and several others saw their lab as a way to help other departments develop ideas and solve problems.

"Disruptive" innovation: The Mayo Clinic wanted to transform the experience and delivery of health care.

Mindset change: P&G wanted to shift to a design mindset across the company.

Perspective change: The ATO wanted to encourage its staff to consider the perspective of taxpayers.

Customer experience: TELUS and the Mayo Clinic wanted to improve the service experience for customers and patients.

Behaviour change: The ATO wanted to discourage cheating.

Collaboration: MindLab wanted to encourage different divisions to work with each other across organizational silos.

Talent: Canadian Tire and others wanted to out-hire Google and Facebook.

System integration: Alberta CoLab wanted to understand systems and find leverage points for innovation.

A well-designed program can achieve several of these goals at once. However, it's fair to say that goals concerned with shifting culture and mindset may take decades, not months or years, to accomplish and require patience and consistency.

How Will You Measure Performance?

What you measure depends on what you want – so it is important to have clarity on what you're trying to accomplish as you think about performance measures. Even with clear goals, there are no perfect measures.

If your end goal is culture change, employee surveys can provide an indicator; Pfizer claimed some success with this. Employee surveys are nevertheless after-the-fact measures of factors that can take a long time to shift. Some organizations deal with this problem by measuring inputs to culture change, such as number of interactions, number of facilitators trained, number of workshops held, etc. The advantage of this approach is that you can at least set quantifiable goals for these things, though you will also need to understand whether they are really having a broader impact on organizational culture.

Innovation output is also not easy to measure. For incremental innovations, you can measure the number of ideas passing pre-set organizational stages in the short term, and market successes in the long term. Disruptive innovations are likely to take much longer to bring about; models like the McKinsey Three Horizons of Innovation in chapter 4 can provide some guidance in looking at measurable activities in the short, medium, and long term.

How, and with Whom, Should You Collaborate?

Organizations are often protective of their secrets, but this shouldn't prevent you from looking outside for ideas. Collaboration – judging from, at least, the people I interviewed – seems to be a defining quality of design thinkers, and almost all of the organizations I spoke to were engaged in some form of external collaboration. The kind of collaboration your organization is ready for will be an important factor as you put your program together.

Collaboration brings in ideas, not just from different perspectives but from different world views. Some organizations – such as P&G and Pfizer – go as far as reaching out to competitors along with suppliers and customers; others collaborate with tech entrepreneurs through communities such as Communitech; still others, such as the Mayo Clinic and MindLab, collaborate with a broader design thinking community.

The benefits of collaboration are evident in strategic alliances, such as that between P&G and Clorox, or in joint coordination of clinical trials between Pfizer and Merck. For Canadian Tire and other companies at Communitech, talent acquisition plays a big role. MindLab's external collaboration is part of an innovation research program and also helps motivate its staff. External credibility – built through programs such as the Mayo Clinic's annual *Transform* conference – can reflect backwards and enhance your reputation within your organization.

The kind of collaboration you engage in will depend on the kind of innovation your organization wants. Disruptive innovation isn't likely to come about unless you invite disruptive perspectives from parties that may initially seem irrelevant – or even a threat. Incremental innovators will be content to work with suppliers and customers within the industry. To change mindsets, you can benefit from communities of practice among design thinkers.

Operational Decisions

Having thought through the major strategic issues in setting up your program, you will want to consider some specific issues that are more operational in nature but have long-term consequences.

What Type of Program Will You Have?

You'll need to think through whether you want to be the provider of solutions – an internal consultant – versus a collaborator and facilitator of collaboration within your organization. You'll also need to work through the conundrum of whether to have a centralized "design lab" or distribute design thinkers like seeds throughout the organization. Each has its pros and cons, and the choices depend on factors such as your organization's goals, its size, its culture, and its innovation strategy. The choices within these dimensions are shown in Figure 7.1.

Broadly speaking, there are four models: think tank, expert hub, independent helper and embedded facilitator. Some of the design thinking programs I encountered were multifaceted and occupied more than one of these spaces.

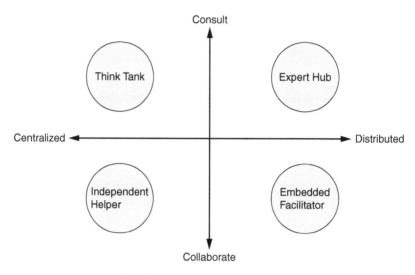

7.1 Models of design thinking programs

There is no magic bullet here, no "perfect" model: each has pros and cons, and each works best in different situations. In setting up your lab, you'll need to think through what works best given your own organization and your goals for design thinking.

Think tank: This model consists of an independent lab that works on organization-wide disruptive innovation projects, such as new technology platforms or new business models. It brings with it independent thinking and provides complete – that is, fully researched and thought through – solutions. The team also may act as an innovation consultant – a SWAT team, if you like – to internal operating units.

This model is most appropriate to disruptive innovation that challenges the organization's current way of operating. Because it is not involved in day-to-day operations, the team can focus on long-term, strategic innovation. It can connect with the world outside the organization, but unlike external consultants, it knows the organization's culture and systems and the chances of ideas being implemented. It provides in-depth expertise in design methods and technology.

This independence is a two-edged sword. Its great advantage is that it allows the team to think differently, but this comes with the risk of cultural isolation – and a dilemma. To get projects implemented, you need to bring operating units into the innovation process, thereby diluting the think tank's independence.

The Canadian Tire lab at Communitech saw itself mostly as an independent innovator, developing technological platforms for departments to take forward and implement. Yet the "one-hundred-kilometre moat" between the lab and head office was a barrier to close collaboration. The Manulife lab at Communitech, however, made a point of staying engaged with its head office while maintaining its independence.

Disruptive projects tend to be long-term in nature, and if you choose to go in this direction, you will need sustained support from top management. You and top management will need to regard this as a venture that will pay out over the long term. With this model, patience is a virtue.

Expert hub: In the expert hub model, design thinkers are embedded in operating units across the organization. They are positioned as innovation specialists, with strong links to the source of innovation expertise – so they are connected with a defined program or a central lab.

Because they are inside operating units, their focus is on incremental innovation and cultural change. Embedded design thinkers in this model can provide operating units with both specialized skills of design thinking and an outward-looking perspective. In particular, they can promote empathy with users and stakeholders.

The cultural home provided by the design thinking program helps limit their assimilation by operating units.

However, it is a challenge for these design thinkers to reconcile their design-based world view with day-to-day business. Short-term internal pressures tend to trump strategic innovation, and embedded innovators can be swallowed up in day-to-day management issues.

The ATO and P&G had elements of this model. In both cases, strong support was provided to the design hubs by bringing design thinkers together across the organization.

If you choose the expert hub model, make sure to provide strong central support. A physical central lab is less important than having an explicit program and building a community of practice across the organization, which meets frequently to share learning and experience. You should also select individuals who are influential within their departments and committed to changing the way they work, and provide incentives and recognition for the independent thinking they bring.

Independent helper: Design thinkers in this model are primarily facilitators who work on request with operating departments to apply design approaches to specific projects. The model consists of a central design thinking unit – a lab – whose role is to help operating units with innovation. Teams from the operating units may come to the lab, or the design thinking team may work on-site if it makes sense for the project. The operating units initiate the projects and own the solutions.

Projects initiated by operating departments under this model will tend to be incremental and limited term. While design thinkers sometimes extend their work into the implementation phase, many are restricted to developing and prototyping ideas. Nevertheless, because the projects are developed in collaboration, there is a good chance that they will be implemented. Successes with these projects can help spread the word and build grassroots support over time.

This arrangement was the starting point for MindLab, though it later became more deeply involved in culture change. At the time, MindLab was concerned that it was not having a deep enough impact on the system. P&G's clay street also operates on this model, as does the TELUS team.

If you choose the independent helper model, be ready to promote design thinking relentlessly. Work closely with operating units to find projects that can showcase your approach. Over time, the momentum for design thinking can build.

Embedded facilitator: Under the embedded facilitator model, design thinkers are operating unit employees trained to facilitate innovation within their departments. Typically, they are not professional designers, but have heard of design thinking and have a personal passion for it.

This is also primarily an incremental-innovation model. The design thinkers have particularly strong relationships within their operating units and can help spread design thinking. Because the innovation work remains within operating units, there is strong commitment to projects. There is also a good likelihood of project implementation: they are close to operational realities and can help troubleshoot problems as they arise.

However, embedded facilitators can too easily be assimilated into operating units and lose the independent perspective that makes them valuable. They can be swallowed up in day-to-day problems and lose the ability to question the fundamentals.

Several programs have tried this model, with limited success. Some reported complete failure – in at least one case, design thinkers "got destroyed" in operating departments. P&G was successful with it, though it depended critically on the quality of the facilitators.

If you choose this direction, make sure to select and train highly competent individuals who can learn to facilitate well. They also need ongoing support, so you will need to check in regularly and, as with the expert hub model, provide them with opportunities to learn from each other.

How Will You Staff Your Lab?

Will you staff the lab (assuming you have a central lab) with professional designers or with people who have different skills? To some extent, this depends on the type of model you choose, but professional designers alone are typically not enough.

Keep in mind that you don't need to be a designer to be a design thinker – and that not all designers are design thinkers. You will need the following kinds of people:

- those who can understand and empathize with the problems faced by managers in operating departments;
- those who are tuned into organizational power centres and politics;
- those who are skilled in design thinking, not necessarily design – though it is helpful to include some designers in the team;
- those who are great communicators and can teach the organization about design thinking; and
- those who are great facilitators and can lead meetings and introduce appropriate methods during the design thinking process.

There was a wide mix of people in the labs I encountered. At the ATO, there was a limited talent pool, and the ATO relied on consultants as it built an internal skill base. TELUS had a mix of designers,

MBAs, and a leader who relentlessly and successfully promoted design thinking. When P&G's design program was launched, it was led not by a designer, but by Claudia Kotchka, a former accountant.

One of the more interesting approaches was that of MindLab, which, as I mentioned in chapter 3, made a point of hiring "nice" people, because of the importance of promoting collaboration within the bureaucracy. As it happened, I was struck by the degree of collaboration and openness I encountered in my interviewees. I put this down to the emphasis on these qualities in the design process itself.

Where Will You Locate, and What Facilities Will You Provide?

Your central lab, if you have one, should provide a "safe space." This means it should not be located in a regular office but in some independent location. However, it should not be too far away either. Good models for this are P&G's clay street and MindLab's studio. All these labs were located in distinctive, dedicated areas, easily – but not too easily – accessible from the main office.

Many labs had humble beginnings. The Mayo Clinic initiative began in a corridor; TELUS, when I visited, did not have a dedicated lab but used whatever meeting rooms were available. Sooner or later, most found funding for a dedicated space.

As we saw in chapter 6, the space itself can be fairly simple. Think of it as a "think space." The main qualities it should have are privacy, so your team can focus, the ability to leave multi-day project work in place, flexibility, plenty of free wall space, and some simple prototyping space. Overall, it should be inviting and feel safe. P&G's "green carpet of safety" at clay street and MindLab's The Mind are nice refinements but in no sense essential.

The location itself may be less important than your team's willingness and ability to conduct workshops on project sites – within operating units – as needed. Apart from the fact that it makes it easier for the operating team to attend, being close to the context of use (such as in a clinical department in a hospital) is often an advantage.

What Kind of Leadership and Governance Will You Have?

Three qualities stood out as important to the success of a design thinking program: support from the top, the ability to work with operating departments, and a strong advisory board.

The role of the leader is critical in gaining top-level support from the organization, in maintaining a pipeline of projects, and in motivating the team. The leader of a design thinking program needs to keep top management on board: this involves not only buying enough "runway" for the program to get off the ground but also taking the opportunity to educate the executive team about design thinking. The leader also needs to be a problem finder who actively seeks out opportunities for collaboration and looks for connections.

Some labs, such as the Mayo Clinic and MindLab, did not rely on the support of a single individual in senior management but established an advisory board that could guide them as they encountered challenges along the way. The advisory board – or as Communitech's Craig Haney called it, the Innovation Council – should comprise external experts on innovation and design thinking, alongside influential individuals within the organization. This approach can help mitigate the problem of leadership changes that have affected design thinking in organizations such as the ATO and P&G.

How Will You Connect with Your Organization? How Will You Build Credibility?

As we've seen, top management support can't be counted on to ensure the survival of your design thinking program. You need to manage your relationship with the organization, and given the Tension of Inclusion, this needs to be approached strategically.

The labs that had cultural or mindset change as one of their goals usually ran regular workshops for employees. Some, such as P&G, trained facilitators and sent them back to brand teams; the experience here, however, was that not everyone was cut out to be a design facilitator. Once they return to their departments, you lose control. The ATO supported its facilitators by bringing them together regularly, on their own time, early in the morning.

Perhaps the most effective way of building internal relationships was through project work. By learning to apply design to projects that were directly relevant to them, managers could begin to see its value; some would follow up and become more involved with the program. The CFI and several others worked this way. The CFI also offered fellowships, so staff could spend periods of several months deepening their understanding of health care innovation.

Reaching out to a broader innovation community also helps build internal credibility. MindLab and the Mayo Clinic CFI had active research programs, and these allowed lab staff to travel and speak at conferences. In turn, this helped build an internal profile for the lab. The CFI's annual *Transform* conference is a major event in healthcare innovation and undoubtedly enhances its profile within the organization.

Some programs, those concerned more with disruptive innovation than cultural change, made less effort to enhance their internal reputation. Their focus was more on the external community than on the internal one. However, even these labs recognized that they had to take on some incremental projects and therefore needed to make the organization aware of their work. This, of course, could generate too much demand for incremental innovation, giving rise to the Tension of Disruption.

Which Projects Will You Take On? Which Will You Say No To?

Design programs typically start with a story, and your first task is to build one. It makes sense to begin with easy wins: projects in which a simple reframe, or introducing the user perspective, can turn existing thinking on its head and lead to simple solutions that anyone might have thought of but nobody did. Stories of such easy wins can help you build credibility.

Design thinking lore is replete with such stories. The Designing Out Crime story from Sydney in chapter 1 is one: by reframing the King's Cross problem from the user's perspective – as a festival, not an opportunity for mischief – the University of Technology, Sydney, team came up with a creative and different response. In a similar vein, the Design Council in the UK worked on improving diabetes care in the context of busy clinics where there was often a deep disconnect between patients and health care workers. The Design Council team used patients' own words to develop a cue-card system for managed conversations.[4]

Organizations are full of situations in which a simple perspective flip can bring dramatic results and give you stories that build your reputation.

Beyond building stories in the initial stages, you should be conscious of the three tensions as you decide which projects to take on – and which to take a pass on. Here are some questions to consider:

Have others tried and failed to solve the problem? (A good thing!)

Is the problem, or problems like it, widely known within the organization? Does it have an impact in several areas?

Is there potential to build a platform for future innovations: a technology, a process, or a collaborative platform?

Is the implementation team open to being engaged in (not just informed of) the development process?

Are you addressing one or more strategic leverage points in the larger system?

Take every opportunity to publicize your work in your organization and, if you can, to the wider world. The websites of MindLab (http://mind-lab.dk/en/) and Designing Out Crime (http://designingoutcrime.com/our-work/) are great examples of how design labs have showcased their work through case studies and detailed discussions of their approaches.

Choices, Paradoxes, and Tensions

In a cramped room in a shared workspace in East Vancouver, I recently met with InWithForward, a "social R&D" group dedicated to "turning social safety nets into trampolines" for families, older people, and people with disabilities. The team had obtained a two-year grant to develop a design thinking lab – later called Fifth Space – in British Columbia, by the end of which it hoped to have obtained core funding from a granting agency or the provincial government.

The group was not naive about the challenges ahead but confident that the project could gain traction. I shared the results of my research with them; one of the team drew a matrix on a flip chart, and we populated it with Post-Its. We looked at best practices, the different models available, and what it would take to succeed. Along with optimism and hope, there was realism. As my journey into organizational design thinking was drawing to a close, it was fascinating for me to be present at the birth of a fledgling program. It caused me to reflect on the choices, paradoxes, and tensions facing design thinkers.

Design thinking has come of age. Judging by the sheer number of organizations that are adopting it, it has caught the imagination of managers across the public and private sectors, across industries and across disciplines.

It is not an easy road, and you should not underestimate the challenge. It needs support from the top, strong leadership, and in-depth understanding. It needs patience and consistent support. The results are not easy to measure. And design thinking programs face the Tension of Inclusion, the Tension of Disruption, and the Tension of Perspective.

With all these obstacles, is it worth it? Yes.

Design thinking can bring fresh perspectives that are overlooked by other approaches. It can help develop empathy, pushing organizations to see things from the point of view of those affected: users, citizens, stakeholders. And because anyone can participate, it can be a vehicle for collaboration across organizational silos.

I emerged from the meeting into heavy rain and a stiff breeze, cursing myself for leaving my Senz umbrella at home. Design thinking, I reflected, is being widely adopted now: it's not quite a deluge, yet – more like frequent showers. The forecast is for more to come.

notes

1. Thinking Like a Designer

1 *The Dream of Making Senz*, 22 February 2013, YouTube video. https://www. youtube.com/watch?v=EnSds7kzqV0. Retrieved 9 June 2016.

2 Cited in Nigel Cross, *Design Thinking: Understanding How Designers Think and Work* (London: Berg Publishers, 2011), 3.

3 Tim Brown, "Design Thinking," *Harvard Business Review* (June 2008), reprint R0806E: 2. Emphasis added.

4 Examples include 5 Whys, user personas, user experience maps, and many others. A great source of tools is Vijay Kumar, *101 Design Methods: A Structured Approach for Driving Innovation in Your Organization* (Hoboken, NJ: Wiley & Sons, 2013).

5 Kees Dorst and Nigel Cross, "Creativity in the Design Process: Co-evolution of Problem–Solution," *Design Studies* 22, no. 5 (September 2001): 425–37.

6 Donald A. Schön, *The Reflective Practitioner: How Professionals Think in Action* (London: Temple Smith, 1983), 102.

7 Kees Dorst, *Understanding Design: 175 Reflections on Being a Designer* (Amsterdam: BIS Publishers, 2006), 177.

8 Richard Boland and Fred Collopy, "Design Matters for Management," in *Managing as Designing*, eds. Richard Boland and Fred Collopy (Stanford, CA: Stanford University Press, 2004), 4.

9 Diego Rodriguez (IDEO), interviewed by author, Palo Alto, CA, February 2008.

10 Marion Buchenau and Jane Fulton Suri, "Experience Prototyping," *Proceedings of the 3rd Conference on Designing Interactive Systems*

(DIS 000) (New York: ACM, 2000), 424–33. http://wiki.cs.vu.nl/swouting/images/e/ef/Experience_prototyping.pdf. Retrieved 29 June 2016.

11 Schön, *The Reflective Practitioner.*

12 Ibid., 81.

13 Dorst and Cross, "Creativity in the Design Process," 434.

14 Schon, *The Reflective Practitioner.*

15 For further details on the history of user-centred design, see my paper, "User-Centred Design and Design-Centred Business Schools," in *The Handbook of Design Management,* ed. Rachel Cooper, Sabine Junginger, and Thomas Lockwood (Oxford: Berg Publishers, 2011), 128–43.

16 Later to be retitled *The Design of Everyday Things* (New York: Basic Books, 1988).

17 Cited in Chunka Mui, "Five Dangerous Lessons to Learn from Steve Jobs," *Forbes* (17 October 2011). http://www.forbes.com/sites/chunkamui/2011/10/17/five-dangerous-lessons-to-learn-from-steve-jobs. Retrieved 15 June 2016.

18 Harry West, "A Chain of Innovation: The Creation of Swiffer [Research Technology Management]," *TMCNet* (14 June 2014). http://cloud-computing.tmcnet.com/news/2014/06/14/7876042.htm. Retrieved 16 June 2016.

19 *Quote Investigator.* http://quoteinvestigator.com/2014/05/22/solve/. Retrieved 19 April 2018.

20 Charles S. Peirce (1903). *Lectures on Pragmatism.* In Peirce (CP) 5.14–5.212. Cited in Gerhard Schurz, "Patterns of Abduction," *Synthese* 164, no. 2 (September 2008): 201–34.

21 Kees Dorst, "The Core of 'Design Thinking' and Its Application," *Design Studies* 32, no. 6 (November 2011), 521–32.

22 *Design Q & A with Charles Eames,* 14 April 2011, YouTube video. https://www.youtube.com/watch?v=3xYi2rd1QCg. Retrieved 24 June 2016.

23 Horst Rittel and Melvin Webber, "Dilemmas in a General Theory of Planning," *Policy Sciences* 4, no. 2 (June 1973): 155–69.

24 Richard Buchanan, "Wicked Problems in Design Thinking," *Design Issues* 8, no. 2 (Spring 1992): 5–21.

25 Charles West Churchman, "Wicked Problems," *Management Science* 14, no. 4 (December 1967): B-141–2.

26 Roger Martin, *The Design of Business: Why Design Thinking Is the Next Competitive Advantage* (Cambridge, MA: Harvard Business Press, 2009).

27 Christian Bason, "Design-Led Innovation in Government," *Stanford Social Innovation Review* (Spring 2013). http://ssir.org/articles/entry/design_led_innovation_in_government. Retrieved 24 June 2016.

28 Josh Hicks, "Can OPM's 'Innovation Lab' Live Up to Its Silicon Valley Billing?" *Washington Post*, 2 May 2014.

29 United States Government Accountability Office, *Office of Personnel Management: Agency Needs to Improve Outcome Measures to Demonstrate the Value of Its Innovation Lab*, (GAO-14–306) (Washington DC: 2014).

30 Lorenzo Allio, *Design Thinking for Public Service Excellence* (Singapore: Global Centre for Public Service Excellence, United Nations Development Programme, 2014), 4. http://www.undp.org/content/undp/en/home/librarypage/capacity-building/global-centre-for-public-service-excellence/DesignThinking.html. Retrieved 27 June 2016.

2. The Adoption of Design Thinking

1 A paper I co-authored with Roger Martin expresses my views at the time: David Dunne and Roger Martin, "Design Thinking and How It Will Change Management Education: An Interview and Discussion," *Academy of Management Learning & Education* 5, no. 4 (2006): 512–23.

2 See, for example, Vijay Kumar, *101 Design Methods* (Hoboken, NJ: John Wiley & Sons, 2013).

3 Jimmy Guterman, "How to Become a Better Manager ... By Thinking Like a Designer," *MIT Sloan Management Review* 50, 4 (2009): 39–42.

4 Bruce Nussbaum, "Design Thinking Is a Failed Experiment. So What's Next?" Co. Design, 5 April 2011. http://www.fastcodesign.com/1663558/design-thinking-is-a-failed-experiment-so-whats-next. Retrieved 18 July 2016.

5 Petra Badke-Schaub, Norbert Roozenburg, and Carlos Cardoso, "Design Thinking: A Paradigm on Its Way from Dilution to Meaninglessness?" in *DTRS8: Interpreting Design Thinking: Proceedings of the 8th Design Thinking Research Symposium*, eds. Kees Dorst, Susan Stewart, Ilka Staudinger, Bec Paton, and Andy Dong (Sydney, Australia: DAB Documents, 2010), 39–49.

6 Brian Ling, "Design Thinking Is Killing Creativity," Design Sojourn, 31 March 2010. http://designsojourn.com/design-thinking-is-killing-creativity/. Retrieved 23 May 2018.

7 Jeffrey Tjendra, "Why Design Thinking Will Fail," Innovation Excellence, 2013. http://innovationexcellence.com/blog/2013/02/25/why-design-thinking-will-fail/. Retrieved 22 July 2016.

8 Donald Norman, "Design Thinking: A Useful Myth," Core 77, 25 June 2010. http://www.core77.com/posts/16790/design-thinking-a-useful-myth-16790. Retrieved 18 July 2016.

9 Lucy Kimbell, "Rethinking Design Thinking: Part 1," *Design and Culture* 3, no. 3 (2011): 285–306.

10 Fred Collopy, "Lessons Learned: Why the Failure of Systems Thinking Should Inform the Future of Design Thinking," Fast Company Design, 7 June 2009. https://www.fastcompany.com/1291598/lessons-learned-why-failure-systems-thinking-should-2inform-future-design-thinking. Retrieved 22 May 2018.

11 Karen Hershenson, clay street external update, 2015. http://claystreet.net/wp-content/uploads/2015/06/clay-street-external-update-Jan-2015.pdf. Downloaded 17 October 2017. *Note:* This content was removed after P&G was contacted.

12 Ibid.

13 Kerry Bodine, "Design: Because Great Customer Experiences Don't Happen by Accident," *Forrester*, 30 July 2012. http://blogs.forrester.com/kerry_bodine/12-07-30-design_because_great_customer_experiences_dont_happen_by_accident.Retrieved22May2018.

14 Yale School of Management, "Founding of SPARC," Design and Social Enterprise Case Series, Case Study #09-034 2010, published 23 November 2010, updated 29 June 2016. http://vol10.cases.som.yale.edu/design-mayo/founding-sparc/founding-sparc. Accessed 9 July 2016.

15 Alan G. Lafley and Ram Charan, *The Game Changer: How You Can Drive Revenue and Profit Growth with Innovation* (New York: Crown Business/Random House, 2008), 105.

16 Alan Duncan and Margaret Breslin, "Innovating Health Care Delivery: The Design of Health Services," *Journal of Business Strategy* 30, no. 2/3 (2009): 13–20.

3. The Tension of Inclusion

1 Yale School of Management, "Mayo Clinic: Design Thinking in Healthcare: Physicians and Designers," Design and Social Enterprise Case Series, Case Study #09-034 2010. http://vol10.cases.som.yale.edu/design-mayo/founding-sparc/physicians-and-designers. Retrieved 24 August 2016.

2 Example from Jeffrey Conklin, "Wicked Problems and Social Complexity," in *Dialogue Mapping: Building Shared Understanding of Wicked Problems* (Chichester, UK: John Wiley and Sons Ltd., 2005), 3–40.

3 Jess Roberts, "Session 2: Evening Powered by PechaKucha," Mayo Clinic Transform Conference 2016. https://transformconference.mayo.edu/speakers/. Retrieved 6 February 2017. Also see Thomas Fisher and Jess

Roberts, "Making Culture Change Possible through Design," Mayo Clinic Center for Innovation. http://blog.centerforinnovation.mayo. edu/2016/09/02/make-culture-change-possible-through-design/. Retrieved 6 February 2017.

4 *A.G. Lafley, Procter & Gamble, Catalyst Awards Dinner*, 31 March 2015. https://www.youtube.com/watch?v=4Yv0RbKAQ1M. YouTube video.

5 *The Evolution of Design Thinking*, special issue, *Harvard Business Review* (September 2015).

6 Helle Vibeke Carstensen and Christian Bason, "Powering Collaborative Policy Innovation: Can Innovation Labs Help?" *The Innovation Journal: The Public Sector Innovation Journal* 17, no. 1 (2012): article 4, 20.

7 David Dunne and Roger Martin, "Design Thinking and How It Will Change Management Education: An Interview and Discussion," *Academy of Management Learning & Education* 5, no. 4 (December 2006): 512–23.

4. The Tension of Disruption

1 These technologies have raised significant privacy concerns. See, e.g., Andrew Marrington, Don Kerr, and John Gammack (eds), *Managing Security Issues and the Hidden Dangers of Wearable Technologies* (IGI Global: Advances in Information Security, Privacy and Ethics [AISPE] Book Series, 2016).

2 Phillip Inman, "Could a Bitcoin-Style Monetary System Spell the End for Britain's Banks?" *Guardian*, 2 March 2016 . https://www.theguardian.com/ money/2016/mar/02/bitcoin-digital-currency-britain-banks. Retrieved 23 September 2016.

3 Graduate Management Admissions Council (GMAC), *Disrupt or Be Disrupted: A Blueprint for Change in Management Education* (San Francisco, CA: Jossey-Bass, 2013); also W. Johnson, *Disrupt Yourself: Putting the Power of Disruptive Innovation to Work* (Brookline, MA: Bibliomotion Inc, 2015).

4 See, e.g., Ernst & Young, *Disrupt or Be Disrupted: Creating Value in the Consumer Products Brand New Order* (2013). http://www.ey.com/Publication/ vwLUAssets/Disrupt_or_be_disrupted:_creating_value_for_brand_new_ order/$FILE/EY_Disrupt_or_be_disrupted_lowres.pdf; Accenture, *Disrupt or Be Disrupted: Prescriptions for Life Sciences in the Age of Digital Medicine* (2015). https://www.accenture.com/_acnmedia/Accenture/Conversion-Assets/DotCom/Documents/Global/PDF/Digital_3/Accenture-Disrupt-or-be-Disrupted-Final-Online.pdf. Retrieved 17 September 2016.

5 Mayo Clinic Center for Innovation, "What We Do." http://centerforinno-vation.mayo.edu/what-we-do/. Retrieved 28 September2016.

6 Nicholas LaRusso, Barbara Spurrier, and Gianrico Farrugia, *Think Big, Start Small, Move Fast: A Blueprint for Transformation from the Mayo Clinic Center for Innovation* (New York, NY: McGraw-Hill, 2015), 47. See also the review of this book: G. Kellerman, "Design or Disrupt? The Mayo Clinic Achieves Patient Care Improvements through Innovation That Is Incre-mental Rather than Disruptive," *Stanford Social Innovation Review* 13, no. 1 (Winter 2015): 71.

7 Yale School of Management. Mayo Clinic: Design Thinking in Health Care. http://vol10.cases.som.yale.edu/design-mayo/founding-sparc/ physicians-and-designers. Retrieved 30 September 2016.

8 Michael Tushman and Charles O'Reilly, *Winning Through Innovation: A Practical Guide to Leading Organizational Change and Renewal* (Boston, MA: Harvard Business School Publishing, 2002).

9 The Balanced Scorecard approach looks at innovation from these four "perspectives." It's interesting and a step forward, but it doesn't link these perspectives causally. See Ronald Jonash and Barnaby Donlon, "Connecting the Dots: Using the Balanced Scorecard to Execute an Innovation Strategy," *Balanced Scorecard Report* (March–April 2007): 1–7. Reprint B0703A.

10 GAO Report to Congressional Requesters, "Office of Personnel Manage-ment: Agency Needs to Improve Outcome Measures to Demonstrate the Value of Its Innovation Lab" (2014). http://www.gao.gov/products/GAO-14-306. Accessed 12 October 2016.

11 Josh Hicks, "Can OPM's 'Innovation Lab' Live up to Its Silicon Valley Bill-ing?" *Washington Post*, 2 May 2014. https://www.washingtonpost.com/ news/federal-eye/wp/2014/05/02/can-opms-innovation-lab-live-up-to-its-silicon-valley-billing/. Accessed 12 October 2016.

12 Mehrdad Baghai, Steve Coley, and David White, *The Alchemy of Growth: Practical Insights for Building the Enduring Enterprise* (New York: Perseus Publishing, 2000).

13 Bansi Nagji and Geoff Tuff, "Managing Your Innovation Portfolio," *Harvard Business Review* (May 2012): 1–9. Reprint no. R1205C-PDF-ENG.

14 L. Keeley, Helen Walters, Ryan Pikkel, and Brian Quinn, *Ten Types of Inno-vation: The Discipline of Building Breakthroughs* (Hoboken, NJ: John Wiley & Sons, 2013).

15 Nicholas Carr, "Visualizing Innovation." *Harvard Business Review* (September–October 1999): 3. Reprint F99501.

16 Jill Lepore, "The Disruption Machine: What the Gospel of Innovation Gets Wrong," *New Yorker*, 23 June 2014: 30–6.
17 Peter Dombrowski and Eugene Gholz, "Identifying Disruptive Innovation: Innovation Theory and the Defense Industry," *Innovations* 4, no. 2 (Spring 2009): 101–17.

5. The Tension of Perspective

1 Danielle Ofri, "Doctor Priorities vs. Patient Priorities," *New York Times*, 27 March 2014. http://well.blogs.nytimes.com/2014/03/27/doctor-priorities-vs-patient-priorities/?_php=true&_type=blogs&_r=0. Retrieved 1 May 2018.
2 Claire Hooker, "Understanding Empathy: Why Phenomenology and Hermeneutics Can Help Medical Education and Practice," *Medicine, Health Care and Philosophy* 18, no. 4 (November 2015): 541–52. http://link.springer.com/article/10.1007/s11019-015-9631-z. Retrieved 8 March 2017.
3 Atul Gawande, "Notes of a Surgeon: On Washing Hands," *New England Journal of Medicine* 350, no. 13 (25 March 2004): 1285.
4 Frido Smulders and David Dunne, "Disciplina: A Missing Link for Cross Disciplinary Integration." Paper presented at the 11th Design Thinking Research Symposium, Copenhagen, Denmark, 13–15 November 2016.
5 Referring to a nineteenth-century allegorical book in which people were unable to see in three dimensions. Edwin A. Abbott, *Flatland: A Romance in Many Dimensions* (New York: Dover Thrift Edition, 1884 [1992 unabridged]).
6 https://creativedifference.ideo.com/#/.
7 Tim Brown and Roger Martin, "Design for Action: How to Use Design Thinking to Make Great Things Really Happen," *Harvard Business Review* (September 2015): 4–10. Reprint R1509C.
8 In progress; for the time being, a good reference is Alex Ryan, "A Framework for Systemic Design," *FORMakademisk* 7, no. 4, art. 4 (2014). https://journals.hioa.no/index.php/formakademisk/article/view/787/1109. Retrieved 9 March 2017.
9 Alex Ryan, "A Personal Reflection on Introducing Design to the U.S. Army," Medium.com, *The Overlap*, 4 November 2016. https://medium.com/the-overlap/a-personal-reflection-on-introducing-design-to-the-u-s-army-3f8bd76adcb2#.kw34zgtdt. Retrieved 23 November 2016.
10 Yotam Feldman, "Dr. Naveh, Or, How I Learned to Stop Worrying and Walk Through Walls," *Haaretz*, 25 October 2007.

11 See, e.g., Peter Checkland, *Systems Thinking, Systems Practice* (Hoboken, N.J.: John Wiley & Sons, 1999); Harold G. Nelson and Erik Stolterman, *The Design Way: Intentional Change in an Unpredictable World* (Cambridge MA: MIT Press, 2014).

12 Alex Ryan and Mark Leung, "Systemic Design: Two Canadian Case Studies," *FORMakademisk* 7, no. 3 (2014): 1–14. www.FORMakademisk.org.

13 Ibid., 12.

6. Reframing Design Thinking

1 Herbert A. Simon, *The Sciences of the Artificial* (Cambridge, MA: MIT Press, 1969).

2 Donald A. Schön, *The Reflective Practitioner: How Professionals Think in Action* (London: Temple Smith, 1983); Nigel Cross, *Designerly Ways of Knowing* (London: Springer, 2006).

3 Kees Dorst, "The Core of 'Design Thinking' and Its Application," *Design Studies* 32, no. 6 (November 2011).

4 See, e.g., Mayo Clinic Center for Innovation: http://centerforinnovation. mayo.edu/design-in-health-care/; Procter & Gamble: http://claystreet. net/creative_process/.

5 Design Kit. http://www.designkit.org/mindsets. Viewed 6 January 2017.

6 Larry Keeley, Helen Walters, Ryan Pikkel, and Brian Quinn, *Ten Types of Innovation: The Discipline of Building Breakthroughs* (Hoboken, NJ: John Wiley & Sons, 2013).

7 Unilever Plc, Unilever N.V., "Deodorant/antiperspirant products with fragrance and encapsulated odour counteractant," Patent #EP 0519531 B1, 1995. https://www.google.com/patents/EP0519531B1?cl=en. Retrieved 5 January 2017.

8 GE Healthcare, "GE Adventure Series: Imaging That Puts Children First." https://www3.gehealthcare.com/~/media/documents/us-global/ products/accesories-supplies/brochures/adventure%20series/gehealth-care-brochure_adventure-series.pdf?Parent=%7BAFE522E5-B54D-4BFA-8343-F41B8A2F69D9%7D. Retrieved January 11 2017.

9 Deborah Adams Kaplan, "Making Imaging Centers Child Friendly," Diagnostic Imaging, 7 February 2014. http://www.diagnosticimaging.com/ pediatric-imaging/making-imaging-centers-child-friendly. Retrieved 11 January 2017.

10 This is the Kolb Learning Cycle: David Kolb, *Experiential Learning* (Englewood Cliffs, NJ: Prentice Hall, 1984).

11 David J. Sill, "Integrative Thinking, Synthesis and Creativity in Interdisciplinary Studies," *Journal of General Education* 50, no. 4 (2001): 288–311.

12 Roger L. Martin, *The Opposable Mind: How Successful Leaders Win through Integrative Thinking* (Cambridge, MA: Harvard Business School Publishing, 2009).

13 Peter Checkland, *Systems Thinking, Systems Practice* (Chichester, UK: John Wiley & Sons, 1993).

14 Birger Sevaldson "GIGA-Mapping: Visualisation for Complexity and Systems Thinking in Design." Paper presented at the Nordic Design Research Conference, Helsinki, 2011. http://www.nordes.org/opj/index.php/n13/article/view/104/88.

15 Amy Kates and Jay Galbraith, *Designing Your Organization: Using the Star Model to Solve 5 Critical Design Challenges* (San Francisco: Jossey-Bass [Wiley], 2007).

16 *Powers of Ten*, 26 August 2010, YouTube video. https://www.youtube.com/watch?v=0fKBhvDjuy0. Retrieved 24 February 2017.

7. Where Do You Begin? Building Your Design Thinking Program

1 Jennifer Rheingold, "The Interpreter," Fast Company, 2005. https://www.fastcompany.com/53060/interpreter. Retrieved 27 February 2017.

2 "SPARC Innovation Program," Wikipedia, last modified 26 February 2017, http://en.wikipedia.org/wiki/SPARC_Innovation_Program; *Mayo Clinic – Evolution of SPARC*, 30 November 2010, YouTube video, http://www.youtube.com/watch?v=6ZPwLie6K-4, retrieved 27 February 2017.

3 Famously attributed to Danish philosopher Søren Kierkegaard in *Journalen* JJ:167 (1843), *Søren Kierkegaards Skrifter*, Søren Kierkegaard Research Center, Copenhagen, 1997, 18, 306. http://homepage.divms.uiowa.edu/~jorgen/kierkegaardquotesource.html. Retrieved 27 February 2017.

4 Colin Burns and Jennie Windhall, *RED Health Report: Design Notes 01: The Diabetes Agenda* (London, UK: Design Council, 2006), 25.

index

Note: **Bold** indicates a photograph or illustration.

www.ingramcontent.com/pod-product-compliance
Ingram Content Group UK Ltd.
Pitfield, Milton Keynes, MK11 3LW, UK
UKHW032119310125
454513UK00001B/44